In spite of
our differences

This book captures the heart of authentic peacemaking – as a lifelong calling, a journey of healing, and growth in humility and courage. Through the story of a pastor who stepped, with deep faith and openness, into communities scarred by war, readers are offered a rare, first-hand insight into the lived experiences of those from 'the other side of the war' – Croats and Serbs. Having lived through the time and places Clive describes – and having worked alongside him – this book touched me deeply and, also, enriched my understanding. It will be a valuable companion for anyone seeking to live reconciliation with God, with oneself, and with others – and for those committed to supporting others and communities on that same path of healing.
A beautiful book about the beautiful life of a beautiful person I deeply admire.

Katarina Kruhonja
Co-founder of the Centre for Peace, Non-Violence
and Human Rights, Osijek and
Right Livelihood Laureate 1998

I welcome this book for its wealth of stories and wisdom from people living and speaking in contexts of war and violence. Their experiences and words speak to our contemporary world and communities facing the challenges of living beside those who are different. The Bench We Share and Touch of Hope show the value of encouraging people to meet and talk with each other. The book outlines stories of hurt and hope, words and workshops that will support peacemakers in their own neighbourhoods and communities. It offers training for non-violence and respectful conversations.

Rev Inderjit Bhogal
past President of the Methodist Conference,
former director of the Corrymeela Community and
recipient of the World Methodist Peace Award

In spite of our differences

Healing the hurts of war

Clive Fowle

Spring View Publications
info@springview.uk

Copyright © Clive Fowle 2025

The right of Clive Fowle to be identified as the author of this work has been asserted by him in accordance with the Copyright, Design and Patents Act 1988.

Scripture quotations are from the New Revised Standard Version Bible, copyright © 1989 National Council of the Churches of Christ in the United States of America. Used by permission. All rights reserved worldwide.

The first verse of 'For the healing of the nations' by Fred Kaan, © 1968 Stainer & Bell Ltd, 23 Gruneisen Road, London N3 1LS, www.stainer.co.uk, is used by permission. All rights reserved.

Cover design by Emma Scott, Kenilworth

Typeset by Candy Evans, Kenilworth

Printed and bound by IngramSpark
ingramspark.com

ISBN   978-1-7398659-6-2
ebook ISBN   978-1-7398659-7-9

Contents

Maps of the former Yugoslavia	1
Foreword	3
A guide to pronunciation in Croatian	5
Timeline	6
Exploring health and healing	8
A call from Geneva	20
Orientation and disorientation	26
Initiation into the work	47
Birmingham	59
The first group visit to Osijek	70
On the move to Leamington Spa	79
From Bench We Share to Touch of Hope	89
Introduction to the workshops	97
Healthy communication, the jackal and giraffe	100
Identity	110
The Wounded Healer	118
Forgiveness	128
Living in a reconciling way	139
A call within a call	149
Sitting together on the bench in the UK	155
Channels of healing	161
Affirmation and a surprise meeting in Osijek	166
Epilogue	175
Questions for group discussion	177
Books I have found helpful on my journey	183
For more information	186

The former Yugoslavia and its surrounding countries as they are today

The United Nations Protected Area (UNPA)
between 1992 and 1996

Foreword

On Tuesday 16 April 1996 at 2pm I arrived by train in Osijek, Croatia. I did not know a soul and I had no idea what would happen during my stay, but I knew I was in the right place at the right time. I met many people who moved me with their stories of the war. I witnessed how ordinary people and non-governmental organisations were making a significant contribution to living in a reconciling way.

Judith Large writes in her excellent book *The War Next Door*:

Second track intervention cannot broker or negotiate international agreements, but it can assist in testing their viability and enabling local populations to improve conditions and take ownership of outcomes.[1]

It was the start of a long journey of learning about the challenges of working for peace and reconciliation in the aftermath of the horrors of war in Croatia, Serbia and Bosnia and Herzegovina.

This book is an account of that journey and I invite you to know more about how Bench We Share and Touch of Hope have empowered people to be peacemakers in their own communities.

In telling the story, I do not give an account of the collapse of the former Yugoslavia. At the end of the book there are some suggestions of books that deal with this. I have quoted from stories of participants of both programmes, Bench We Share and Touch of Hope. Some of the stories are in our companion book Wounded in War, Touched by Hope. I urge you to read these very moving stories. To protect individuals, and at their request, some names have been changed or withheld.

I am grateful to the many people who have been part of this momentous journey, some of whom remain anonymous. Others have participated in workshops. The Community for Reconciliation has played an important part and I am grateful to its workers past and present and to those who have served on committees. Thank you to my wife Ann, Adrian, Mark and

---

[1] Large, Judith *The War Next Door* p48 Hawthorn Press 1997

In spite of our differences

Jonathan for their support, especially when I have been away conducting workshops in the region. So many people have inspired me that it is difficult to single out any individual without offending others. Thank you to Katarina Kruhonja, Nena Arvaj and Snježana Kovačević for their forbearance, wisdom, skills and language expertise. Thank you to Judith Halliday for her colleagueship and facilitation skills. Thank you to Alex Dickie, Andrew Fagg, Dr Paul Kybird, Ron Lyall and Penny Osborne. Thank you to Jericho Writers and Dexter Petley for his perceptive comments and Candy Evans for agreeing to publish the book. Thank you to the Methodist Church and to those who have donated towards the work.

I am dedicating this book to Dušanka Ilić who invited me on to the bench in 1996 to share in her work. When I first started communicating with Dušanka, we did so by fax. She always finished her faxes with the words, *Peace and Love in spite of our differences (Palisood)*. I trust that she has found the peace for which she worked so hard. May she rest in that peace.

Clive Fowle
September 2025

A guide to pronunciation in Croatian

A a a in father

B b as English b

C c ts in cats

Č č ch in church

Ć ć roughly tj

D d as English d

Dž dž J in John

Đ đ roughly dj

E e e in bed

F f as English f

G g as English g

H h ch in loch

I i e in he

J j y in yes

K k as English k

L l as English l

M m as English m

N n as English n

Nj n in news

O o o in not

P p as English p

R r rolled

S s ss in bless

Š š sh in shy as Dushanka

T t as English t

U u oo in food

V v as English v

Z z as English z

Ž ž s in pleasure

Timeline

Yugoslavia and world events		Clive Touch of Hope
Tito becomes Prime Minister of the FPR of Yugoslavia	1945	
	1946	
	1947	Born in Kingston upon Thames, Surrey
Yugoslavia expelled from the Soviet bloc	1948	
	1949	
...		
	1961	
	1962	Learnt German
	1963	
...		
	1970	
Tito introduces a rotating presidency to share power between nationalities	1971	Learnt Russian
	1972	
	1973	Trained as a pastoral counsellor
	1974	Community work in Victoria, London
	1975	
...		
	1979	
Tito dies	1980	Trained as a Methodist minister
Unrest begins. Kosovo demands status as a full republic	1981	Formed links with East Germany
	1982	
	1983	Ordained as a Methodist minister; began ministry in Milton Keynes; formed link with Leipzig
Sarajevo hosts winter Olympics	1984	

Timeline

	1985	
	1986	
Emergency security measures introduced in Kosovo	1987	
	1988	
	1989	Began ministry in Acocks Green, Birmingham
	1990	
	1991	
Recognition of Croatia and Slovenia by the European Community; The Bosnian referendum on independence takes place, fighting breaks out; Part of Eastern Slavonia is under Serbian rule; May: Sarajevo under siege	1992	
	1993	
	1994	
July: Srebrenica massacre November: Dayton Peace Accord Exhumation of the mass grave site at Ovčara near Vukovar	1995	
	1996	First visit to Osijek
	1997	
Fighting spreads to Kosovo NATO attacks on Serbia	1998	
	1999	Graduated with MA in Peace Studies from Bradford University
	2000	Trained as a mediator
Milošević handed over to the International Criminal Tribunal for the former Yugoslavia at The Hague	2001	
	...	The work continues

Chapter 1

Exploring health and healing

Filip prepares to leave his house in Osijek. As he kisses goodbye to his wife Sonja and their two boys, Nika and Ivan, he feels a mixture of apprehension and excitement. He is about to drive to Ilok to join a Dodir Nade (Touch of Hope) workshop.

Bench We Share was good. With my fellow veterans, we learned how good it is to share our feelings about the war. It was hard at first, because as a boy I was never encouraged to talk about my feelings, but Dušanka encouraged us all to say how we felt. Once underway, our words tumbled out. Tears came too as we recalled our difficult experiences. I imagine Dodir Nade will be the same.

Filip had heard about Dodir Nade through the Centre for Peace, Non-Violence and Human Rights in Osijek.

Ilok is Croatia's most easterly town and sits on the bank of the Danube on the border with Serbia. It marks the boundary of the EU. It takes well over an hour and a half to drive there. It is February and the sky is blue. It is also frosty and cold as Filip takes the long, straight, treeless road out of Osijek, past the small airport at Klisa which is busy only in the summer when there are flights to the coast. He passes through several villages with signs offering eggs and vegetables for sale. He drives through the outskirts of Vukovar, past destroyed houses and some signs of rebuilding. He passes the station building, bombed in 1991, still awaiting restoration. The water tower, which took more than 600 hits in the conflict, looms up before him as he drives into the centre of town. He heads for Sotin, past the memorial inscribed with the names of missing and departed people. He is sad as he passes the turning to Ovčara. He cries for all the victims, and the suffering they endured.

From here to Ilok, the road is deserted, the traffic is light as he passes through Opatovac, where a camp for refugees was hastily erected in 2016. At that time, the area was full of people fleeing from Syria, Afghanistan and Iraq. They had travelled across the water to Greece and onwards through Serbia to Croatia. The road passes

Exploring health and healing

vineyards dating back 2,000 years to Roman times, undulating with twists and turns as the car winds its way through Šarengrad. This area is characterised by picturesque houses and views over the river Danube. The descent to Ilok and the Danube hotel is spectacular, finishing with a long line of trees along the driveway to the hotel. The hotel, known for its good cuisine, is spacious, with tables outside and a lovely workspace. From the car park, Filip gazes across into Serbia, watching the boats and barges travelling up and down the river. Cars, lorries and coaches go back and forth over the bridge, in and out of the EU into Serbia. It is a tranquil scene that helps create a peaceful atmosphere.

Ilok had been part of the Ottoman Empire until 1697 and there are reminders of Ottoman rule in the walls within which the old town is set. The calmness of the Danube belies the fact that the area was occupied in 1991 by the Yugoslav National Army (JNA). An ultimatum was given to non-Serb residents to leave their town to make room for Serb refugees.

Other participants arrive one by one. After checking in with the hotel, everyone makes their way to their rooms before coming downstairs to meet one another and the team. Filip says, 'I've been looking forward to meeting you Clive. Dušanka told me a lot about you and your commitment to working with us in Croatia. I am sorry my English is not so good.' I introduce myself in Croatian and secretly congratulate myself for doing so. Some participants come up to Judith and me, asking questions in perfect English. This puts my feeble attempts to speak the language into perspective. I congratulate them on their English and discover they have been learning from a young age.

Introductions

The workspace is next to the dining area and everyone drifts over to the refreshment table. They help themselves to fruit juice, water, fruit tea or coffee and snacks. Filip eyes Judith and me as we ask participants to sit in a circle. 'Just like Bench We Share,' he thinks to himself as he sits down. 'We always sat in a circle; we are all equal.' Filip learns that Judith is a mediator from Coventry, offering mediation and conflict support and coaching for neighbour disputes. She was brought up in South Africa and has been coming here with Clive for many years. Listening to me, he learns first that I am the coordinator of Dodir Nade; second, that I am a minister in the Methodist Church; and thirdly that I work as a mediator with Judith. Filip asks: 'What is the Methodist Church Clive?'

'Well, that is a big question. How long do we have?'

Filip laughs and says, 'I look forward to hearing more.'

I continue. 'The Methodist Church of Great Britain is a protestant denomination in Britain and the mother church to Methodists worldwide, including Serbia and Macedonia. It was founded in the 18th century by John Wesley who was a priest in the Church of England. Originally the Methodists were to be a renewal movement within the Church of England. The word 'methodist' was a nickname given to new Christians who were very 'methodical' in the way they lived out their Christian discipleship.'

Calling everyone together, I say that 'our goal this weekend is to broaden our understanding of Health and Healing. We shall look at how we can live healthily in our own communities.'

Filip is on familiar territory as he remembers how Dušanka used to run her sessions. I announce that we shall decide what things are going to help us work together in a constructive way. Other members of the group make suggestions.

The rules of the session – *pravila radionice* – are then displayed on the wall. Listen to each other, respect one another, talk only from our own experience, which is known as 'I speech' *(ja govor)*. Everyone has the right to pass, which means if a person does not want to take part in an activity, then that is fine. Confidentiality is important.

Filip fumbles in his pocket for his mobile phone as everyone agrees to put phones on silent mode or switched off. A timetable is agreed upon and then the round of introductions begin. 'What now?' Filip exclaims. He must choose another person and find out about that person, then introduce them to the group as if he is that person, stating their reasons for coming to Dodir Nade.

The participants start their exchange. Everyone becomes very animated and engrossed in conversation, so much so that I struggle to stop them talking. A hush falls on the room as one by one each is introduced. Some speak in English, but to ensure everyone understands, Snježana and Nena act as interpreters.

Exploring health and healing

Filip looks round to his right and has already realised the woman sitting next to him is Serbian.

I can tell from the way you speak that you are Serb. In fact, I can't remember a time when I have heard so much Serbian being spoken at a meeting. What brings you to this session?

I am Viktoria, 38 years. I live in Berak. I work as a housing officer in Vinkovci. Filip, you represent for me the enemy, a fighter on the opposite side. But I am tired of living as enemies and want to think about how we can better live together. I am married with two children. I heard about Dodir Nade through Luč (Light). It is a group working for peace in my area. How about you?

I'm Filip, Croat and 45. I live in Tenja. It hurts me that you use that word 'enemy', but that was true and I was the enemy. But I don't have to be the enemy now in this session. I used to be a bus driver until I served in the army. Now, I'm unemployed and I have PTSD. I went to a Bench We Share workshop with Dušanka and other war veterans. Then when Dušanka became ill, I heard about Dodir Nade. I long for better health. I have a very patient partner Lidija, who deserves medals for putting up with my moods and anger. She cares for my two lovely boys Nika and Ivan'

Both Viktoria and Filip struggle as they introduce each other to the group. Viktoria becomes emotional when speaking as if she is Filip, a Croat, and Filip is tearful as he introduces Viktoria, a Serb.

Judith introduces Nena.

I am Nena. I live in Osijek and have been working with Dodir Nade for a long time. I studied at Osijek Bible College and have worked with the Centre for Peace in Osijek. I worked in Mostar Bosnia with both Christian and Muslim communities. I trained as a mediator and work with the Osijek Mediation Service. I am married with two daughters. My husband Teofil fought in the Croatian army and has been a participant on Dodir Nade.

Clive introduces Snježana.

I worked with Centre for Peace in Osijek for many years and with Touch of Hope. I am married with a son and daughter. I attend the Pentecostal church in Osijek.

Filip loves the next part as Nena announces a game to help remember each other's names. A small ball is thrown to a member of the group who says their name. That person then throws the ball to someone else who in turn says their name. When everyone has participated, the whole sequence is done in reverse. The ball travels everywhere across the room, narrowly missing people's heads while we just about remember each other's names. Everyone laughs.

What does a healthy person look like?

After the introductions, Filip is feeling more relaxed, but tenses up again as Judith and I explain we are not going to be standing at the front of the room giving lectures. Instead, we are hoping for active participation from everyone, in all our activities. In our first task, what does a healthy person look like? Filip finds himself in a group with Viktoria.

Filip is tall, well-built and is the first to stride forwards and take a sheet of paper. He says to Viktoria

What would my fellow comrades think of me fiddling around with pieces of paper and drawing? In any case, I can't draw, but I do help my kids draw at home.

His voice booms out over everyone in his group, calling his fellow group members to gather together.

I honestly don't know where to begin as I can only show you what an unhealthy person looks like. I can't sleep, I get nightmares, I get flashbacks to the war. When I hear bangs in the street, I jump because I think it is the sound of gunfire. I can't relax and I have a short fuse and get angry very quickly. I shout at my wife and my kids are afraid of me. I am a nervous wreck. I am too reliant on tablets.

Viktoria, slim and of slight build, sidles up to Filip, 'For God's sake Filip, just get on with doing what Clive and Judith have asked us to do. Do I draw a man or a woman, young or old, tall or thin?' She begins drawing a man with two legs, but Filip remonstrates saying: 'Why not draw a man with only one leg? He can still be healthy, even although he only has one leg.' Viktoria nods in agreement and continues. Two groups have drawn a woman and one group has drawn a picture of a man who has no legs.

Filip presents the picture to the main group. The image of the man with no legs provokes a lot of comment. The point of the

Exploring health and healing

picture is ably made. Filip says, 'The man lost his legs in the war and although he cannot walk, he can still be healthy in his mind. Besides, there is a chance he may have some prosthetic legs.'

I put forward a definition of health. 'Health is the ability to respond in a mature way to life as it is.'[2] Filip warms to this.

It is about how we have to change and adapt when life throws up challenges in our face. We cannot bring back the past, but we can shape the future through the way we communicate with one another. This is what Dušanka kept saying to us, and she was right.

The line of health

Both Filip and Viktoria feel awkward when they are asked to assess how healthy they are. Viktoria turns to Filip and says: 'Clive is asking us to give ourselves a score out of 10 and then we are all going to line up outside. This could be embarrassing, but shall we be honest?'

For war veteran Filip, it is the first time he has sat down to really think about his health. 'How do I assess my health?' he asks himself, 'For a start I am a physical wreck. I used to be so fit when I joined the army and could run the 10,000 metres in a fast time. Now I am incapable of running. I am obese and I cannot sleep. Memories of the war keep coming back and I have nightmares most nights. Spiritually, I see very little point in life. I feel generous if I give myself a score of 1.' But just then he remembered something that Dušanka had said to him: 'Be gentle with yourself,' she'd said. 'Do not be violent with yourself.' 'For that reason, I give myself a score of 3.'

Viktoria is less reticent about giving herself a higher score, settling on a 6. She explains to the group:

I am less outgoing now than I used to be, and more anxious. I think the war has left me with less confidence and I find it hard to trust people. Physically, I am fit, but mentally and spiritually I feel bankrupt.

The group has worked hard this morning. Apart from a brief break for drinks and snacks and a quick smoke for some people, the pace has been quick. I produce a box of Cadbury Roses

---

[2] Dr Michael Wilson *The Hospital – A Place of Truth* 1971

chocolates. I try to do this for every workshop and explain the Cadbury story, of how the firm was founded by members of the Society of Friends. I explain the Quakers are heavily involved in peace work. 'No need to feel guilty, as these chocolates are peace chocolates,' I say. (I do not mention that times have moved on, and that Cadbury is now owned by Mondelez International). It is time for lunch, cold meats, fish, salads, vegetables followed by fruit pie, cream and ice cream. There is time for a quick stroll into the village or along the shore of the Danube. I decide to walk into the village and on the way back to the hotel I bump into Filip who is struggling with the uphill walk. 'You see what I mean when I said I used to be so fit. I could have run up this hill a few years ago.'

We sit down and reflect on the morning session. Filip tells me he is seeing a psychiatrist for PTSD and takes many tablets. The psychiatrist recommended Dodir Nade because there would be more opportunities for talking and healing on Dodir Nade than if he were simply relying on him as a doctor. 'No pressure for us then,' I reply. He laughs and embraces me as we hasten to the hotel. I am pleased the psychiatrist recognised the value of our programme.

After our lunch break, having devoured large quantities of chocolate, it is time to work again. The session after lunch in any workshop is often called the graveyard shift. To wake us all up, we play a game in which Nena stands in the middle of the room and invites everyone wearing glasses to change places. As half of the group scrambles across the room, Nena quickly sits down. The person left standing becomes the leader and invites people who are wearing blue to change places. The game moves fast and everyone laughs as people are desperate to get a seat until we run out of reasons to change places.

The healing of the paralysed man

After that burst of energy, Filip is exhausted, collapsing onto a chair. He comes to life again when the next task is to consider the story of the healing of the paralysed man, as told in Mark 2:1-12. I read the story through and then invite the group to act it out. If I suggest role play at a church in the UK, people generally hide under a table. There is no such hesitation today. On the contrary, they await instructions eagerly. Very quickly, Viktoria enthusiastically offers to play one of the friends who bring the paralysed man to Jesus. After some thought, Filip volunteers to play the paralysed man. He thinks to himself: 'Shall I be honest, or shall I pretend I am well when I am not? But I can't tell anyone else yet. I am paralysed but I want to be healed.'

There is a mood of anticipation as the drama begins. Jesus is teaching. People are listening intently. But then everyone looks up and there is a lot of commotion as the owner of the house gesticulates, complaining about the mess caused by four people lowering the man through the roof. Slowly, the paralysed man is brought in by his four friends to the feet of Jesus. Jesus forgives his sins, at which point the murmurers protest and Jesus addresses them. In front of them all, Jesus commands the man to get up, take his mat and go home. The atmosphere is electric. The man gets up and walks. Those who are amazed let out squeals of delight and wonder, while those who protest continue to moan. There is a carnival atmosphere as people cheer loudly and clap for joy at the healing.

But Filip, playing the paralysed man, is in tears. He cannot move for exhaustion. Viktoria hugs him and we take a break. Filip is dazed and overwhelmed. When others try to talk with him, he is incoherent, his words burbling out like a child. After the break, Filip listens attentively to Judith, me and others as we reflect on the role play, asking the question: 'In what ways are we paralysed?'

I am an atheist, but I can't explain what has happened in the role play because I feel so different now.

'In what ways are you different?' I ask him.

When Jesus asked me to get up, I suddenly felt stronger mentally than ever before. It was as if I do not feel as helpless and powerless as I have been. I have a big problem, which I have had ever since I was in the army, and it has torn apart my marriage. It upsets me to talk about it.

Judith and I encourage him to take his time speaking to the group.

Before I joined the army, I used to enjoy a drink with the lads. As I was a bus driver, I was always careful not to drink too much if I was on duty the next day. But when I enlisted it became the

In spite of our differences

norm to drink more and more with my mates. Then it was not just beer but spirits as well. We were just having a good time and somehow the drink helped me get through the days. I never felt I was a heavy drinker until Lidija commented on how I had changed as a husband and father. She told me I was moody and at times incoherent. I was shocked when she told me that the children were afraid of me. I realised I was becoming a slave to alcohol as I was getting more and more dependent on it. No matter how hard I tried to drink less, the alcohol had got a hold on me and I was hooked. The strange thing was that when Clive read the story of the paralysed man, I identified instantly with the sick man. When we were told that he was being let down through the roof, I saw myself in him and remembered when I had to be carried home by my colleagues, not because I was ill, but because I was drunk. I am sick because I am addicted to alcohol. Somehow, when I stood up in the play, I felt that things can be different. I was given hope.

The group falls silent and two people immediately walk over to embrace him. 'We can help you recover,' they say.

'Thinking about the story,' I continue, 'how does it help us to understand health and healing?' Viktoria is the first to speak.

I think for me, the role of the friends is important and shows how we all need support from friends and family.

I have been thinking a lot about friendship. I really liked being one of the friends who brought the paralysed man to Jesus. We were full of expectation that the paralysed man would walk again. He was so lucky to have people to bring him to Jesus. I have lived in Berak for many years. It is a small village and we accepted each other with no regard to nationality. We all helped each other. The fighting started and suddenly some people started avoiding those from 'the other side'.

My husband Igor is a Croat, working as a heating engineer, knowing many people because of his work. He and I have lived in the area for over 15 years. We had many friends and we were in and out of each other's houses. In my work as a housing officer in Vinkovci, ethnicity was never an issue. Many of my friends were Croats, but since the war some avoid me in the street. There were several times when they shouted outside my door to leave the village. What has happened since the war is that communities are divided and some people feel pressurised into taking sides. A Croat came to me and said that he would like to come to my house. I am afraid of what others may think as they tell him not to have contact with me. Can I trust my friends any more just because of who I am, a Serb?

Nena interjects:

People say that the loss of trust between people is one of the biggest casualties of the war, but here is the place to begin trusting each other.

Viktoria continues: '

When people are betrayed as they were in the war, is there really any hope that trust can be regained?

It is time for our main meal of the day and we drift over to the dining room for a marvellous spread of meat, fish and vegetables. We tuck into our food and we are all deep in conversation with one another. I am asked about my own interests. On hearing that I love buses and trams, Filip reminds me he has been a bus driver.

Later that evening, Filip catches me and tells me more of his life story. I find out he was brought up in Tenja, a village just south east of Osijek. Life was hard with his brother and sister, money in short supply. Like so many people, his parents kept chickens and a pig and grew vegetables. Filip had a great wish to travel and became a long-distance bus driver on the route to Germany. In the summer of the late '80s, the coach firm began excursions to Spain and Filip was offered the job of driving to the Costa Brava. He was very happy in this job but became more and more worried about the deteriorating situation in Kosovo in 1989.

Becoming very emotional, he explained how, to his horror, fighting had broken out in 'his own back-yard', the villages he knew from childhood. He felt compelled to enlist and defend his people.

I need to tell you, Clive, that Tenja has a very dark history. A camp was established in 1942 resulting in 3,000 Jews being deported to Auschwitz and Jasenovac. There is even a memorial to the camp on the road from Tenja to Osijek. I needed to defend my village, so I volunteered and enlisted in the army. I saw a lot of dreadful things but I was committed to defending my homeland. One night I

In spite of our differences

became really depressed and thought about that camp for Jews in the village. I suddenly realised that, by being violent, I was no better than the people who sent the Jews to the gas chamber. I was singling people out according to their nationality and sending them to their death. I began to question myself about what I was doing and felt guilty. I developed PTSD and started to have nightmares and flashbacks of the war.

After such a busy day, my head is spinning and it is time to touch base with my co-workers, to review the day and plan for the final session.

What does a healthy community look like?

The group is up early in the morning, before 8am, enjoying the winter sunshine on the Danube where all is quiet. Filip is strolling along the river bank. He and Viktoria fall into conversation.

I really miss my husband Igor. He has suffered so much. At school when I studied German, we read the story 'Metamorphosis' by Franz Kafka. It is about a man who wakes up in the morning to find that he has changed into a dung beetle. Igor says he feels like that beetle, less than human, because his former friends despise and ignore him because he is married to a Serb. It would be good if he could come to these meetings and find the support he needs.

Filip replies:

I love being on these meetings, but I feel I said too much yesterday in the group about my problem with alcohol. I feel now that people will be watching me to see if I drink too much. Look, Clive and Judith are calling us together for the last lap this weekend.

On joining us, he asks: 'What have you in store for us Judith?'

'An action-packed morning for us all,' Judith replies. 'We have done a lot of talking, acting and playing games but this morning we want to tap into your artistic talents.'

Filip sighs, and mutters to himself. 'Not more drawing?'

Judith, sensing what Filip is thinking, continues.

'We are thinking this morning on what makes a healthy community. We want to create that in miniature, using clay, paints, model making and words. We shall have lots of paper and a lot of room to create this healthy community.'

Exploring health and healing

Without further ado the group accepts the challenge and starts working together, in silence.

Slowly, the collage takes shape. The sky is first black with clouds at one end of the paper, but as an artist moves from left to right, the sky lightens until deep blue on the right. A mosque is positioned in the centre of the paper and an Orthodox church is put next to it. Filip makes a model of a house, cuts out pictures of people and puts them into the house. He wants to portray the paralysed man being lowered in, so the house is roofless. Viktoria has lots of little houses with big fences around them, except one, in which two people embrace.

There are a lot of green spaces with flowers, trees and people having picnics together. There is a big light shining brightly, which denotes the organisation Luč, meaning Light. Luč provided the opportunity for people to come together to work for peace and reconciliation. Somebody adds a Roman Catholic church next to the mosque. Families are playing football with their children and there are lots of playgrounds.

We have prayer for healing. Everyone gathers in a circle and I give a short message of hope quoting James 5:13-17. I pray for each person, laying hands on each head and saying, 'may God bring healing and peace to you in body, mind, soul and spirit.'

The quiet of these moments speak volumes. After the prayer, the group sits for several minutes reflecting on the experience.

Tired but satisfied, Filip drives home to Osijek. As he turns the corner to his house, he sees his children Nika and Ivan. They rush up to him and he sweeps them into his arms. 'We have missed you dad,' they say. Holding back the tears, Filip says, 'I've missed you all as well but I am home now, and I have had a good weekend away.' Going into the house he notices a bottle of rakija, but it remains on the shelf.

For Viktoria the homecoming is no less emotional. She is excited and wants to share with Igor what has happened but Igor is worried. They hug and Viktoria asks what is wrong. His workmates have seen Facebook posts from Viktoria about the weekend and have been rude and cynical about Dodir Nade. Viktoria concludes that 'we have a long way to go if we are going to be reconciled, but we must try.'

Chapter 2

A call from Geneva

Let us come out today on the roads to peace.
Voicing regrets with our whole being...
Quenching the fire of hate by love,
Sending messages of peace to the world.[3]

The queue at passport control at Belgrade Nikola Tesla airport in Serbia moved very slowly. My colleague Judith and I had been expecting to stand in the 'all other countries queue', but we were still in the EU line as the first Brexit Day, 29 March 2019, had come and gone. My turn came at last and the dour faced young officer took my passport. *Dobar dan*, I said to no response. His face, at first impassive, gradually became very agitated. Thumbing through the pages of the passport, he took his pen and crossed out one of the stamps, his face black with anger. The stamp was from my visit to Kosovo a few years earlier. I did not argue or make any comment. *Hvala lepo*, I said. The same happened to Judith. This was not the first time there had been an issue about a stamp from Kosovo. Crossing from Croatia to Serbia before, the Serbian border guard was furious and waved his hands in the air, shouting expletives, informing me in no uncertain terms that Kosovo is Serbian.

Kosovo declared independence from Serbia in February 2008. The USA, UK and other European countries recognise its independence, but Serbia, backed by Russia, does not. Neither do ethnic Serbs in Kosovo. Travel between Serbia and Kosovo remains fraught for non-Serbs.

If you enter Kosovo at the capital's airport in Pristina, or from Albania or Macedonia, the Serbian authorities regard this as entering Serbia illegally. Non-Serb travellers cannot cross from Kosovo into Serbia if there is no valid Serbian entry stamp. It is thus common practice for Serbian border guards to write the word

---

[3] *Bozidar Golik (Bole)* Touch of Hope participant *Wounded in War, Touched by Hope*

A call from Geneva

'cancel' over a Kosovo stamp or, as happened to my colleague and me, simply cross it out.

The incident reminded us the status of Kosovo is one of many unresolved issues as a consequence of the break-up of Yugoslavia. NATO-led peacekeepers and EU rule-of-law monitors remain in Kosovo. I have been there twice, once in 2003 and then in 2015, but the Touch of Hope programme has not done any work there. Our work is concentrated on Croatia, Serbia and Bosnia and Herzegovina, three of the six republics that made up Yugoslavia.

The border control incident was soon behind us as we made our way to Novi Sad. Our mission that weekend was full of promise. The Touch of Hope team had trained up nine people to be facilitators to lead workshops. Three of them were now preparing to deliver training on health and healing to a new group of 12 participants, most of whom were from Serbia. Judith and I were travelling there to help prepare them.

I had come a long way since 1994 when I made my first contact with peace work in the region.

Faced with 5,000 hungry people, Jesus is introduced by the disciple Andrew to a boy carrying five loaves and two fish. Jesus takes them and distributes them to the crowd.

Some time ago, I identified with that boy. I was committed to building peace but did not feel I had much to contribute. I said to God, something like, 'I don't have much but here is what I have.'

Early on in life I had become convinced, as John Paul Lederach would later write, that 'reconciliation is the mission, the organising purpose around which we understand and see God's work in history.'[4]

I inherited a love of languages from my father. He was fluent in French, Italian and German. He read Goethe in the vernacular over breakfast. I developed a deep interest in Europe, studying German and Russian at Portsmouth Polytechnic, a period in which I came to faith.

I participated in London's CND rallies, but you could not gain an understanding of the 'enemy' there, so I began to attend meetings of Anglo-Soviet societies. Many years later my father,

---

[4] Lederach JP *Reconcile* p126 Herald Press 1999

In spite of our differences

who allegedly worked for MI5, confessed he had been very concerned – convinced these societies were infiltrated by the KGB.

In the summer of 1968, I worked in West Germany, spending all my hard-earned cash on a trip to West Berlin. At that time, the Soviet army invaded Czechoslovakia. Fear and panic spread through both East and West Berlin. I took a tour bus into the East, driving through the infamous Checkpoint Charlie, and had my copy of The Times confiscated at the border. My impression of East Berlin was one of darkness, decay and gloom, yet our guide, a young attractive blonde woman, was full of pride and optimism about life in the German Democratic Republic, dismissing the Federal Republic and the West as decadent.

I took great interest in the Cold War and learned about the conditions for faith communities behind the Iron Curtain. By the 1980s I'd become a Methodist minister. There was much talk of the Russian Threat to world peace. I felt it was important to develop church and civic links with Eastern Europe.

On 9 November 1989, the crossing point from East to West Berlin was opened up. Thousands of people streamed through the frontier. Just weeks beforehand, I had been in Leipzig for the regular 5pm Monday service at the Nikolai Kirche in the heart of the city. At the service, men and women spoke passionately about craving the basic human right to travel freely anywhere in the world. They wanted to be free of surveillance from the Stasi secret police. After the service, people poured out onto the streets to demonstrate for change. In the beginning they had worn a symbolic badge on their clothes denoting swords into ploughshares (Micah 4:3), but those men and women who wore such badges were targeted by the Stasi. When I looked carefully at people's coats, I could see where badges had been taken off. On one occasion I witnessed men, women and children surrounding the Stasi buildings with a ring of candles. These were ordinary people, who made a lasting impression on me.

I did not witness the fall of the Berlin Wall on the 9 November, but I was in the city not long afterwards and chipped away a piece of masonry to keep. To this day it serves as a prompt to chip away at the walls that divide us in our communities and in the wider world.

A call from Geneva

Footprints

Out of this experience came the resource network, Footprints, formed by two other ministers and me. We supported congregations in making church links between East and West Europe. We published a newsletter, organising visits and exchanges.

In September 1989, I was newly stationed in Birmingham at Acocks Green and St Michael's Anglican/Methodist church in Hall Green. I chose to introduce services of healing by the laying on of hands. Years before in Portsmouth, I had attended Jubilee Pentecostal church, where every week Pastor Thomas said, *Are any among you sick? They should call for the elders of the church and have them pray over them* (James 5:14-15). Members of the congregation would come to the front and have hands laid upon them as they were anointed with oil for healing. What impressed me so much was the lack of fuss and drama. It was a normal part of the weekly service. At Acocks Green we did the same, challenging ourselves to become a healing community. We formed a healing team and the evening healing services became very popular, with men and women travelling across Birmingham, even in bad winter weather, to get to the service.

The Anglican *Alternative Service Book* of that period had a striking prayer, *Make whole both men and nations*. 'How does the Church go about that kind of ministry?' I asked myself. The hymn writer Fred Kaan lived in Acocks Green and we often met in the local supermarket. I love these lines from his hymn, *For the healing of the nations*:

Lead us forward into freedom;

from despair your world release,

that, redeemed from war and hatred,

all may come and go in peace.

Show us how through care and goodness

fear will die and hope increase.[5]

Singing it, I realised that the hurts of war and conflict could be dealt with only by in-depth ministry. I knew I needed to be better

---

[5] Fred Kaan © 1968 Stainer & Bell Ltd

In spite of our differences

informed about how to work for peace and reconciliation. I saw an advertisement in *The Big Issue* for an MA course in Peace Studies from Bradford University, to be held at Woodbrooke Quaker College in Birmingham. There was a man from Osijek in Croatia on the course. He told me how the war had started in Croatia and now had spread to Bosnia and Herzegovina. Sarajevo was currently under siege and there was fighting in other parts of Bosnia, too. My ears pricked up when he spoke about the desperate need for people to bring opposing sides together and work for reconciliation.

I wrote to the World Council of Churches in Geneva, asking how local churches could support reconciliation work in the former Yugoslavia. The reply came quickly by phone, remarkably from John, the uncle of one of my stewards.

'It is very rare,' he said, 'to receive a letter from a British Methodist church. You ask about supporting reconciliation work in the former Yugoslavia? Go to Osijek. Make contact with the Centre for Peace, Non-Violence and Human Rights.'

John wished me well and put down the phone. This was a significant moment for me. The call to go to Osijek came in such ordinary circumstances; I had been cooking tea for the family. Yet I suppose that in a way it was typical; some of the disciples were fixing fishing nets when Jesus called them to follow him.

I began corresponding with the Centre for Peace, Non-Violence and Human Rights. I circulated their newsletter to publicise their work locally and raised money for their work. Then, in 1996, came my time for a three-month sabbatical.

On any sabbatical, it is important to spend some time away from home. I had already identified that I wanted to explore the theme of reconciliation. What I really wanted to do was to visit the Corrymeela Community in Northern Ireland. I was inspired by their work of bringing together members of both Protestant and Catholic communities.

Yet something very strange happened. No matter how much I tried to visit Corrymeela, that door did not open. I sent letters and rang several times asking if I could stay at Corrymeela and share in some of the activities. The replies were always polite and reassuring that they would make arrangements for my stay.

A call from Geneva

However, nothing happened. A visit to Corrymeela had to wait until 20 years later, in 2016.

'When the Lord closes a door, He opens a window', they say in the film *The Sound of Music*. Or as an Old Testament writer puts it, *for everything there is a season, and a time for every matter under heaven* (Ecclesiastes 3:1). The window which opened looked out to Croatia. However, the staff at the Centre for Peace, Non-Violence and Human Rights in Osijek were frustratingly silent, too. I did not know what to do. Time was moving on quickly. On the point of near despair, a letter popped through the door. I looked at the stamp; the letter was from Osijek and it was an invitation from the Peace Centre. The way had become clear and the decision to go was made that day.

In preparation for the trip, I met the World Church Secretary for Continental Europe at the Methodist Church's headquarters in London. Though he affirmed my calling, he had some sharp words of challenge.

Is an English Methodist an appropriate person to build bridges between those who have been hurt by war in Croatia? Are you sufficiently aware of all the subtleties of this conflict? Have those injured invited you to help them?

These words caused a lot of heart searching. I found it hard to find an answer to the question which was, bluntly, 'What's it got to do with you?' I had to settle, in that moment, on Phillip's words to Nathanael, *Come and see* (John 1:46), which I felt were echoed in the invitation from the Centre for Peace. I had to be open to what God was leading me into.

At Heathrow Airport I met the husband of one of my wife's oldest friends who was working in Brussels. We chatted briefly. 'What will you be doing in Croatia?' he asked. 'I have not got a clue but I know it will be good,' I said.

Chapter 3

Orientation and disorientation

I was on the front line.
One step
Away from death.

Bullet in the chamber,
Finger on the trigger,
20 something of November –
The memory still lingers.

Wartime posting,
Let it be remembered:
3/21-2263-13/91

Osijek, 11 September 1991[6]

It has been estimated that the subsequent war-induced mass exodus from Osijek reduced the population by one half. The sound of singing was heard from cellars and shelters at nightfall in attempts to drown out the sounds of war. People emerged each morning to sweep up broken glass and plaster from pavements.

Orientation

I have a vivid recollection of arriving in Zagreb at midnight and sharing a taxi with an American who was involved in humanitarian work. The fact that he seemed to know his way round Zagreb only increased my apprehension. Outside the glass-fronted Hotel Dubrovnik at 1am, I could not find the entrance door. Then, when I had difficulty getting into my room, I felt stupid and uncomfortable being in Zagreb at all. What was I doing there, in this country where everything appeared to be normal?

[6]Vlado Đurđević Touch of Hope participant, Wounded in War, Touched by Hope Community for Reconciliation 2012

Orientation and disorientation

I explained to a member of the hotel staff my purpose in coming to Croatia, and she informed me that there had been a rocket attack on the Ban's Palace in 1991. Seven people lost their lives in attacks on the city in 1995. Other than that, compared to where I was heading, Eastern Slavonia, the damage to life and property was small in the capital.

Over the years of travelling to Zagreb I have grown to love this bustling European city and its efficient tram network. The staff at the hotel were very helpful in directing me to the Glavni Kolodvor, (Central Station) which meant catching a number 6 tram. A member of the hotel staff had said that in travelling to Osijek I would be going to the Austro-Hungarian part of Croatia.

Osijek

I caught the 10am train and arrived in Osijek at 2pm on Tuesday 16 April 1996. On the train were two stewardesses who worked for Croatia Airlines who could not understand why I was travelling to Osijek. They said it was 'the end of the line, where people are a bit mad down there.' What did they mean? Did this refer to the violence of the war, or was it simply a reference to the 'superiority' of living in or near Zagreb, the capital city, as opposed to living in Slavonia?

I loved the long, slow journey, taking everything in. We stopped at so many small stations, where staff chatted to passengers as they got on and off the train, all the way to Osijek, the end of the line. I took a taxi to the Centre for Peace, Non-Violence and Human Rights, very reassured by the taxi driver who told me the workers 'do very good work at the Centre.'

After the capital Zagreb and the coastal cities of Split and Rijeka, Osijek is the fourth largest in Croatia. Osijek is situated in the region known as Eastern Slavonia. Its population has been reducing in recent years, down from a peak of around 130,000 in the early 1990s to fewer than 100,000 today.

I discovered there are three parts to the city; Lower Town, Upper Town and the old Town. On that first visit to the city, I found that people were very friendly and helpful. They directed me to the river Drava where I enjoyed the spring sunshine, walking along the riverbank past the huge Hotel Osijek with its bars and restaurants. Small boats were moored up in a backwater and everything seemed pleasant and normal. I went back and forth over the huge pedestrian bridge. On the other side was a grassy area, a children's playground and paddling pool, which was deserted. My walk back then took me along the bank until I came to Tvrđa (The Citadel).

I was now in the Old Town. From the riverside walk, I could see the remains of what was a star fort, a wall and parts of the former bastions. I remembered the words of the receptionist at the Hotel Dubrovnik in Zagreb, that in coming to Osijek, I would be visiting the Austro-Hungarian part of Croatia. Here before me was an example of a Habsburg fortress built in 1715, after the defeat of the Ottomans.

I continued my walk into the inner town. Formerly consisting of military buildings, before me stood a lovely old square surrounded by university buildings, the Museum of Slavonia and St Michael's Church, built by the Jesuits on the foundations of a Mosque in 1748. Every Friday at 11am the bells are rung recalling the exact time the town was liberated from the Ottomans in 1687. In the middle of the square stands a votive column erected in 1729 which acts as a memory of the victims of a plague and as a protection against the curse of further plagues. However, today the monument was boarded up as a reminder of the recent fighting in the old town. The monument had not protected the population from the curse of the war.

From the twelfth century, Osijek had been an important trading centre, attracting both merchants and craftspeople. As the population grew, Osijek developed as the cultural, industrial, educational and administrative centre for Slavonia, with a university, theatres, exhibition halls and art gallery. While returning to the City Centre via tram, or strolling through the city in those early days, I could see signs of the recent conflict. Pock-marked buildings, the presence of Organisation of Security and Cooperation in Europe (OSCE) vehicles along with UN troops and vehicles. There was an air of normality until I spoke with people about what happened in 1991. Then, people became tearful as they recounted what it was like living under attacks from planes, from Yugoslavian National Army (JNA) forces and Serbian paramilitaries.

Orientation and disorientation

I passed the Red Fico monument, a red car behind a tank. As tanks rolled on to the streets in 1991, a resident parked his red Fiat (Fico) on the street to block them. The first tank continued on its route, and they both remain today as a tribute to defiance. The artillery bombardment of the city of Osijek by the JNA took place between August 1991 and June 1992. There were 800 deaths and a large proportion of the population left the city.

The Catholic Church of St Peter and Paul is just off the Ante Starčević square in the centre of the city. It has the second tallest spire in Croatia (90m) and is built in the style of a German Cathedral. It is often referred to as a Cathedral and was conceived by a German architect with the encouragement of Josip Strossmayer, a Croatian politician, Roman Catholic Bishop and benefactor, born in Osijek in 1815 in what was then the Austrian Empire. Strossmayer also gives his name to many streets in Croatia. The Cathedral took a bad hit when JNA planes struck it and killed two people.

I was welcomed warmly by members of the Centre for Peace. Marina and Branka made arrangements for me to stay with the sister of Katarina Kruhonja, co-founder of the Centre for Peace. The following morning Katarina's brother-in-law walked with me into the centre and then along the riverbank. It was glorious April sunshine. We stopped for a coffee in one of the bars overlooking the river and he reflected on the horror of what had happened in Osijek, the hatred that had been stirred up against Serbs by Croats, and against Croats by Serbs. He went on to say that the worst part about it for him was how ethnically mixed families had been torn apart by the violence.

From early on in my conversations, I realised many people had family all over the former Yugoslavia. Someone would say he was originally from Macedonia but his wife was born in Bosnia and still had family there. Another woman I met was from Hungary and her husband was Serbian, which meant they frequently visited both countries. Yet all these people lived in Osijek. As people mentioned places, I tried to picture where they were and what life was like for them before and after the war. I was constantly looking at maps of the region. I also felt it was important to network with other groups working for reconciliation, for us to work in partnership with them.

Disorientation

However, I felt uncomfortable, stupid and ignorant of the whole situation in Osijek. I struggled to understand the language. I had studied Russian at college and recognised some Croatian words because Croatian and Russian are Slavic languages, but I felt out of my depth.

Moreover, the war had moved on from Croatia and Bosnia. The presidents of Bosnia, Croatia and Serbia had all agreed to a US-brokered peace deal in Dayton, Ohio. From 1992 in Croatia, a cease-fire was in force until 1996, when the area was under the control of United Nations Protection Force (UNPROFOR). UNPROFOR was deployed in United Nations Protected Areas (UNPAs) which were set up to ensure that a lasting cease-fire was maintained. UNPAs were areas where Serbs constituted a substantial majority of the population and where inter-communal tensions had led to armed conflict. A UNPA had been established in Eastern Slavonia in Baranja, which is in the north-east part of Croatia, three sides of a triangle bordered by Hungary, the river Drava and the river Danube. The river Danube forms the state border with Serbia. Baranja is a lowland region with agriculture and the food industry being the main industries, the largest of which is Belje.

Belje goes back to 1697 and its strapline is 'Delicatessen with a taste of tradition', the skill and tradition passed down for generations. One of its most famous products is Baranja Kulen which is a smoke-dried product made from pork meat from its own pig farms with peppers and spices added. Its other well-known products are the wines produced locally, the most famous of which are those produced from a type of grape known as Graševina, which is native to Baranja.

It is thought that the name Baranja comes from the Slavic word *bara* which means bog or marsh. It has 38 settlements, the largest of which is Beli Manastir, near the border with Hungary. Darda and Bilje are large villages. Baranja stretches also into Hungary so that the whole of Baranja is effectively the land between the Danube and Drava rivers. The train service runs from Osijek through Bilje and Darda to Beli Manastir, some trains connecting

Orientation and disorientation

with a cross- border service to Pécs in Hungary. Housing is very distinctive in this region. People grow their own vegetables and fruit, keeping chickens and the occasional pig. Until the 1991/2 war, 50,000 people of mixed ethnicity lived there, Serbs, Croats, Hungarians and other nationalities. The census held just before the war in 1991 showed a population in Eastern Croatia of 42.49% Croats, 35.11% Serbs, 6.7% Hungarian and 22% Other (Slovak, Czech, Albanian, Montenegrin, Ruthenian). Place names can be found in Hungarian, Croatian and Serbian languages. The Yugoslav National Army (JNA) invaded Baranja on 24-25 August 1991.

The UNPA stretched to Vukovar and the surrounding area. Vukovar, an attractive town on the river Danube, was completely devastated in 1991. The name comes from the Vuka river and the Hungarian word var, which means fortress. Because of its position on the Danube, it became an important centre and harbour for shipping, both import and export. However, in 1991, it received notoriety in other ways for mass slaughter and destruction. It became an important focus for our work, but we would have to wait some time until we worked there. When I mention to people outside Eastern Slavonia that we hold workshops there, I notice people become sad and tearful. The fall of Vukovar in November 1991 was a watershed moment and has been described as the worst atrocity of the war in Croatia. Tensions came to a head between Croats, 44% of the population and Serbs, 37%. Politically all the talk was of independence for Croatia, which then provoked a backlash from Serbia. Consequently, Serb paramilitaries and the JNA moved into the town with hundreds of tanks and soldiers. The town was pounded mercilessly from the air and ground. The famous water tower, which had been built in the late 1960s, was hit more than 600 times during the siege. It had been home to a restaurant with wonderful views of vineyards over the Danube. I spoke to many people who had dined in the restaurant.

The population did the best they could by sheltering in their homes with little or no power supply and lessening stocks of food. The devastation came to a head on 18 November as people of all nationalities took refuge in the town hospital. The Red Cross had planned to evacuate the hospital as the JNA had agreed with the Croatian government. However, 263 men and 1 woman, mostly

In spite of our differences

Croatian but also other non-Serbs, including wounded patients, hospital staff, political activists, civilians and journalists, were taken to agricultural storage hangars at Ovčara, about three miles south of Vukovar where they were held, beaten and tortured. They were subsequently taken in small groups and executed at a remote site. Their bodies lay undiscovered until September 1996 when 200 bodies were exhumed, of which 194 were identified. The bodies of the very popular Radio Vukovar journalist Siniša Glavašević and his technician Branimir Polovina were among them. Siniša had managed to continue broadcasting from the radio station during the bombardment. An anonymous tip-off located the grave. An obelisk marks the spot, along with 200 small bushes. It has a sculpted dove and the inscription: 'In remembrance of 200 wounded Croatian men defenders and civilians from the Vukovar hospital who were executed in the Greater Serbian aggression against the Republic of Croatia.'

The storage hangars at Ovčara were used for a few months as a transit camp for Croatian prisoners. A memorial centre was opened in the hangar in 2006, housing the possessions of those who were murdered, their photographs intermittently projected on to the walls of the centre. Vukovar hospital was rebuilt and there are reminders of what took place in the bombardment, such as a crater on the ceiling of a corridor where a JNA shell fell but did not explode. There are rooms furnished in the way things were in the war. Along the basement corridor is a timeline of events of November 1991. According to statistics, around 2,300 soldiers and civilians died defending the town. 2,600 people disappeared. Many were taken off to camps.

The International Criminal Tribunal for the former Yugoslavia has brought several people to face justice for the Ovčara massacre.

From 1996 the United Nations Transitional Administration for Eastern Slavonia (UNTAES) took over. UNTAES discovered that Eastern Croatia had the highest concentration of mass graves and missing persons in the country.

I was very confused about the situation in Osijek and Baranja. I wanted to visit the region of Baranja and Vukovar, but was told I had to get permission from the UN, which took a long time. Besides, I had no official status in the region.

Orientation and disorientation

My discomfort about being in Osijek was made worse because I felt I had come at the wrong time to visit the Centre for Peace. There was a constant stream of visitors and the staff members were tired. I also heard criticism of people who had come from abroad and promised much, but in fact gave very little. I vowed that I did not want to become such a person. I went to visit the Evangelical Theological Seminary (ETS) in Osijek. It was founded in 1972 in former Yugoslavia and its first home was a church basement. It was one of the few Protestant theological schools to open under communism anywhere in Eastern Europe. Restrictions in other countries behind the Iron Curtain made ETS an important centre in the region for theological study. Alongside the college is the Evangelical Pentecostal Church, housed in a former Synagogue, which is over 100 years old. It has the Star of David at its top on the front of the building. I heard that Jews were rounded up in World War 2 outside the synagogue and sent to their death in Jasenovac, Croatia and Auschwitz. The Jewish community was happy that the Church bought the building and occasionally the Jewish community has meetings there.

I met many students and took part in their worship. The tunes were all well known to me from singing hymns and songs back home, but the words were in the Croatian language. I looked forward to meeting a member of staff, a woman from abroad who was there with her husband, but I was put off by her questions.

'So why have you come? What are you doing here? What do you intend to do here? Who invited you to come?'

I felt increasingly uncomfortable with her questions. I felt as if I was being interrogated. Her persistence in asking these questions challenged me to ask myself, why had I come, what right had I to be there? Was I needed? My answers did not seem convincing to her as she persisted in bombarding me with questions. I told her I had heard about the Centre for Peace and had been contacted by the staff and invited to come and see the situation in Osijek for myself. I was relieved to note that on hearing the word 'invited', she ceased her aggressive questioning. I came away angry and wished I had had the courage to ask her why she had come to live in Osijek and what right had she to be there? I also came away from the Seminary wondering what it had been like for the churches during the bombardment of Osijek.

In spite of our differences

The walk from the Seminary into the city centre was very long and happened to be along a tram route. To my delight I came to the tram depot and bus garage and began to cheer up at the sight of trams as I set foot into the depot. I have a deep interest in trams, buses and trolleybuses. What was also interesting was the fact that trams had been shipped in from Germany to replace trams that had been destroyed in the war. The German trams still bore German advertisements and notices. The experience of trying to visit tram and bus depots in Eastern Europe in the past had been very negative as governments have been wary of allowing foreigners to photograph vehicles and premises because of security concerns. However, having reassured the staff I merely wanted to see the trams and buses in the depot because I was a devotee, I managed to negotiate my way into the depot and was soon rewarded. Right at the back was a vintage tram being lovingly cared for by an elderly staff member. He was pleased to see me and greeted me warmly and showed off the vintage tram, his pride and joy.

'I am getting this tram ready for the tourists,' he told me. 'They will come back one day and when they do, this vintage tram will take them for rides once more.'

His belief that things would eventually turn to normal was refreshing. He reminded me of the prophet Jeremiah buying the field at Anathoth (Jeremiah 32). Jerusalem is under siege and almost falling to the Chaldeans and Jeremiah buys the field at Anathoth in the belief God will restore his people to the land. My stay at the depot revitalised me and I continued my journey into town. But the 'third degree' I had received at the Seminary still bothered me and I began, once again, to feel uncomfortable at being in Osijek.

Katarina Kruhonja

Just when I felt I had made a huge mistake in coming to Osijek, I met Katarina Kruhonja, co-founder of the Centre for Peace, Non-Violence and Human Rights in 1992. Katarina's mother had just died, and she invited me to meet her family who were gathered for prayer in the family home. I was staying with Katarina's sister and brother-in-law. I was privileged to be part of this family time together to take strength from each other and from God in their time of grief.

Orientation and disorientation

Katarina Kruhonja had been a doctor of Nuclear Medicine at the local hospital. She had given up this work to become involved in peace work. I remember vividly that first meeting as she described how she felt she had been too passive in her reaction to the conflict in Osijek and that she had to do something to counter the violence and loss of life and property in her city and in the region. She took the step of faith and took responsibility for her actions.

She later wrote in her annual report of the Centre for Peace:

The beginning of my personal dedication to peace work and reconciliation could be placed in the moment when I became aware of my part of responsibility for what was going on – it was in summer 1991. I became aware that my own passivity towards politics was a factor which also contributed to outbreak of the war.

Katarina is a devout Roman Catholic whose opposition to war arose out of her religious beliefs.

I was aware of the breadth of the Centre's work and its international contacts as I talked with Katarina and other staff members. A volunteer from Holland was working from the office. The Centre had moved into new premises after being based initially in the old town in the Museum of Slavonia. It acted as a focal point for peace activities in the area, initiating and coordinating activities, making it a compulsory place to consult for anyone wishing to work for peace in the area. I was beginning to understand the reasons why it was considered essential that I visit there. It acted as a resource and information centre, offering legal aid in human rights, while opening up communication and building trust and cooperation between those who are in conflict. The activities benefited all people from all ethnic groups in the area, but certain groups of people such as teachers and community leaders (people with influence in their community) became involved, in the hope they would influence others in their own work for peace in non-violent ways. Sister Mary Evelyn Jegen, a US university professor, has written a very inspiring account of the Centre for Peace with the apt title 'Sign of Hope'[7].

---

[7] Jegen, ME Sr Sign of Hope Life and Peace Institute 1996

In spite of our differences

Meeting Katarina was very significant and we have shared many workshops together.

A major influence on Katarina and the Centre for Peace was Adam Curle. His influence still resonates today among people who had been involved with the Centre for Peace in those early days. He is respected for the way he developed community approaches to dealing with Post Traumatic Stress Disorder. At an early age he was interested in the psychological effects of trauma and the work he did on healing the psychological wounds of war was groundbreaking. He was a strong advocate of community initiatives involving local people who ensured that the international and national peace agreements made at the macro-level would work at the local level. He made links with psychotherapy and peacemaking and used mediation. He was instrumental in creating a culture of peace in Osijek. He was much admired, and still is, for his wide experience in working internationally in mediation, and for his wisdom and encouragement of peace work in Osijek. He had wide experience internationally on three continents. He himself was profoundly influenced by Katarina and the work of the Peace Centre. He was the first Chair of Peace Studies at Bradford University in 1973 and other colleagues from Bradford became involved in the Centre for Peace. Sadly, I never met him but I am challenged by his writings. I particularly warm to the way in which he combined his spiritual beliefs with academic learning. I like the way in which he stresses that conflict is here to stay but the important point is how we respond to conflict.

However, I did meet with four other important people.

Dušanka Ilić

The first was Dušanka Ilić, Cica for short. I had asked the Centre for Peace staff if I could meet a leader of a project. I felt uncomfortable asking this as I knew the staff were tired. However, Peace Centre staff explained to Dušanka there was 'this man from England' who was interested in knowing more about the work of bringing together people in conflict and asked if she would be prepared to meet him.

That meeting turned out to be a decisive turning point in my life, having had lasting consequences for the reconciliation work and my ministry as a whole.

Orientation and disorientation

Dušanka had worked as an elementary school teacher in Darda since 1972 and could not see me until the close of school in the afternoon. She bustled her way into the Peace Centre and over several cups of tea we talked and talked about why I was in Osijek and what I hoped to achieve. I said I was there to learn about the situation in Osijek and be as supportive as I could to the work of the Centre. She was a bit wary of the fact that I was a Methodist minister as she said she was an atheist. I said I was not there to proselytise but simply to learn about the situation and support reconciliation work. Dušanka was apologetic about her English and asked me to be patient, saying there were three kinds of English: 'English English, American English and Dušanka's English.'

We related to each other very well immediately and she was extremely patient with me as she explained the geography of the area, saying that we were now in Eastern Slavonia. I asked her where Western Slavonia was, and we joked about where East and West began and ended. After sharing who we were and why I was there, she turned to me and described her passion. With great enthusiasm she told me about Bench We Share, (Zajednička klupa). I was enthralled.

She explained the significance of the bench in Baranja. The name of the project Bench We Share, Zajednička Klupa, is based on the tradition of a Turkish word and custom Divani, meaning 'evening gatherings on benches in front of village houses'. She told me that as one travelled through Baranja there were many houses with a bench in the front. Before the war, people of different ethnic backgrounds would sit on the bench drinking tea, coffee or something stronger, putting the world to rights. She explained not every house had a bench but neighbours would come and join each other on the bench. Before the days of TV, radio and newspapers, the bench would be the place to catch up with the local gossip and news. There were no reserved seats, passers-by were welcome. People from the other end of village would come, or those in a hurry simply stood beside the bench.

The war came and this picture of harmony and trust was shattered. The benches became empty. She explained that the goal of the project was to enable men and women from different ethnic

In spite of our differences

groups to sit on the same bench together, to begin to trust one another again. For Dušanka, the central question was, 'How can we live together in peace and tolerance respecting our differences?' Dušanka told me about how the project had developed. She spread a huge map over a table, the facts and figures at her fingertips.

During the conflict, 30,000 fled from Baranja to Osijek, which suffered considerable damage to its industry and homes. After that, Croats and Hungarians began to run away from Baranja and their homes. 10-15,000 Serbs came from other parts of Croatia and Bosnia and occupied houses.

In 1994 the territories of Baranja, Eastern Slavonia and Western Sermium were occupied by the Yugoslav National Army (JNA) and so people from Osijek were unable to enter these territories. Meetings of displaced families, neighbours and friends were organised in the Hungarian town of Mohács, just over the border from Croatia. In 1994/5, meetings had been organised for over 1000 individuals from both sides of the United Nations Transitional Authority in Eastern Slavonia (UNTAES) border. The project was initially called The Meeting House. The name Bench We Share was given to the project in summer 1996 when it was possible to enter Baranja under the protection of the Transitional Administration of the UN (UNTAES).

Dušanka described the aims of Bench We Share as opening up communication between conflicting parties and to increase tolerance in Baranja, and re-establish trust between residents through the use of mediation between neighbours, friends, colleagues, temporary residents and owners of houses.

She added that it was essential to have peace education; education in non-violent resolution of conflict in schools and in local communities. She told me how she was seeking to establish and empower local peace groups.

Because Dušanka lived and worked in Baranja, she knew many people and was trusted by Serb and Croat alike. She remembered as a child seeing the benches in front of the houses in the villages. 'They had a special meaning for the people,' she said, 'because they were the meeting places, places for talking and they were beautiful, peaceful talks.' The bench had a special place in her heart and mind. The project was her passion.

Orientation and disorientation

I came away from our meeting profoundly moved. I said I looked forward to learning more and attending one of her workshops, providing the participants allowed me to come. We parted, promising each other to keep in contact.

Krunoslav Sukić

Krunoslav (Kruno), was a teacher of philosophy and literature, Katarina's partner in setting up the Centre. Kruno described himself as a non-believer, seeing the Church as part of the problem and not as part of the solution. He has been described as 'an ardent seeker of the truth in a way reminiscent of Gandhi.'[8] What I appreciated about Kruno was his awareness of the responsibility that we all have as individuals to protect human rights and the rights of all living creatures. He was particularly active in non-violent direct action when people were being forced out of their homes. It was always a real joy to meet Kruno because he was always so open to everyone whom he met. Although critical of the Church and its response to the war, he was keen to hear of my involvement as a Methodist minister and my motivation for wanting to know more about the work of Centre for Peace. I loved his warm embrace. I remember his words, 'welcome Clive, come and sit for a while and let's drink coffee.'

Together with Katarina, Dušanka and Kruno set the tone for the ethos of the Centre; both religious and non-religious are involved. Everybody who shared its aims and objectives was welcome to be a member.

Martin Kovačević

Martin was a teacher by profession, now living in Friendship Village, a camp for 2,000 displaced persons at Čepin just outside Osijek. Martin and his wife Stojanka had been displaced from their home in Bilje and were now living in basic accommodation in a prefabricated building consisting of two rooms, one of which served as a combined kitchen, living room and bedroom. The Centre for Peace had a major role in working with displaced persons, with an emphasis on empowering Croats who had been forcibly expelled by Serbian forces.

---

[8] Barbara Mitchels has written a detailed account of his life and influence on the work in her book *Love in Danger* Jon Carpenter 2006

In spite of our differences

There were 34,000 displaced persons in Osijek, some of whom were in bad living conditions, losing their sense of identity with nothing to occupy their time. The prevailing discourse of hatred in the media did not help their recovery.

It was to be sometime later that I visited Martin and his wife in the camp, but I heard how, using his horticultural experience, he was teaching some families to grow flowers and vegetables in small garden areas, the produce sold locally in the village. Martin realised gardening was a constructive way of occupying people and make money as well. With the help of Centre for Peace and the UNHCR they acquired plastic greenhouses and, with donations, the gardening grew.

Martin also worked with children full of anger whose parents had suffered traumas. Improving their communication skills, he helped them think positively about themselves and each other.

Charles Tauber

Charles ran Coalition for Work with Psycho-trauma and Peace, holding workshops and working with individuals suffering from Post-Traumatic Stress Disorder. Charles was Jewish and from the USA and trained as a doctor in the Netherlands. He lived and worked in Vukovar and was fluent in Croatian. He breezed into the Centre for Peace and it was lovely to be able to talk with him about his work. He was interested to hear why I had come. As well as meeting Charles, I met a Dutch volunteer at the Peace Centre and the three of us went to Bonus restaurant for a lovely meal. At the time in the UK there was an embargo on eating beef and the waiter commented on this as I chose a beef dish. It was mentioned that the head of the UN Mission in the area, Mr Klein, was a frequent visitor to the restaurant and lo and behold, in he walked and the staff immediately fussed over him. It was good that we had almost finished our meal and did not need much more attention now that Mr Klein had come. I was eating in good company.

On my last day in Croatia, which was spent in the capital, I went with Charles to a very moving place, The Wall of Bricks, which was situated outside the headquarters of the UN Peace Mission. It was a monument to lost and missing people, both civilians and soldiers. It was later dismantled and the bricks formed the basis of a memorial in the city's Mirogoj Cemetery. After this,

Orientation and disorientation

Charles and I attended an international conference in Zagreb about the treatment and torture of men from the region in camps during the conflict. The title of the conference was 'Medical and psycho-social help for male victims of sexual maltreatment in the war in the former Yugoslavia'. It was organised by the Medical Centre for Human Rights in Croatia.

I listened to and read harrowing stories in the conference brochure. I heard different speakers on how difficult it was to work with male victims of the war as they are often slow asking for help and dealing with their traumas.

A story from the Vukovar area

For example, here is a story from the Vukovar area.

I was born in 1958 in Vukovar and I am a Croat. I was captured on 18 November 1991. I surrendered to save the lives of civilians and was registered by the International Red Cross. I was taken by the JNA to Ovčara by trucks along with other prisoners. We were met by Chetniks[9] from Vukovar and Negoslavci who requested the command over the prisoners and started kicking and beating them with sticks and rifles. We were taken to Sremska Mitrovica (in Serbia) and guarded by reservists and prison guards.

Psychological tortures were the worst. They would separate the most corpulent man, jumping on him and threatening while we had to watch all that. Some of the prisoners were taken out. We heard gunshots and they never came back,

Prisoners had to make confessions under coercion, because of which some of them ended up at the Court Martial. They were all beaten and interrogated for days, thrown unconscious back into the room. They had to sign impossible confessions like the raping of Serbian women and massacre of children.

---

[9] The Chetnik movement was a Serbian nationalist and monarchist paramilitary organisation. It was formed as a resistance movement against the Ottoman Empire in 1904 participating in the two Balkan wars and two world wars. Several modern Serbian paramilitary organisations formed in the 1990s after the break-up of Yugoslavia and they chose the name 'Chetnik'. They considered themselves to be a continuation of the Chetnik legacy.

In spite of our differences

Chetnik Zeljko came from Vukovar. He came every weekend and beat our people after taking them outside or in the hallway. We heard moans and cries and he had a list of people he was looking for. There were others who used to come with him, but they were wearing masks. Nevertheless, we recognised some of them by their voices.

There was another Chetnik who came but did not hide his face as he stepped over people, kicking them and hitting them with his hands, sticks and chairs, whatever he could get his hands on.

The worst experience was when I was ordered to spread my legs with hands behind my back and Chetniks were running into me and kicking me across my genitals. They were beating me like that for as long as they felt like it and I was in terrible pain.

The horror of the conflict had caught up with me and I began to feel physically sick at what I heard. I spoke with one of the organisers of the conference about possibilities of forgiveness and reconciliation and was met with a blank stare and the comment, 'How can you expect anyone who has experienced torture to even think about forgiving, let alone utter the word?'

I felt as if I was being put in my place as somebody who had come from outside the situation and did not have a clue about how to deal with the issues. There is a time and a place to talk about forgiveness and reconciliation, and this was obviously neither. I was out of my comfort zone.

The time came for me to leave Croatia. I had come to the end of my sabbatical. As I boarded the Croatia Airlines plane to London, my head was spinning with the conversations with Dušanka and other members of the Peace Centre, the admin staff, Katarina, Kruno and Charles. This visit had ignited my passion for peace work and I wanted to be involved with the work in Osijek. In my mind I could see pictures which had been shown at the conference that day, of men being held in camps. Many questions were going through my head: Can victims of torture recover from their trauma? Do those who inflict torture ever show remorse? How does one support families of those who have become victims of torture? How can the Church support both victims and perpetrators? However, I was also thinking about re-entry back into circuit life. I was looking forward to seeing my wife and sons and sharing with them my experiences in Croatia. Although I had valued being in Germany in the middle of the sabbatical, somehow the Germany work was receding to the back of my mind. The potential for the peace work in Croatia had come to the fore.

The person sitting next to me on the plane was a writer and journalist who had been doing research for a book, a history of Croatia soon to be published. Subsequently, I read it avidly and found it very helpful in understanding the history of the country. In fact, I am continually consulting the history books. We had a lot to talk about on the journey back to the UK. He was particularly interested in the fact that I was a Methodist minister and in how I wanted the churches in the UK to engage with the issue of reconciliation.

Back home but disorientated

I came back from my first visit to Osijek very overwhelmed by what I had experienced. I felt burdened about the need for the healing work. I was excited about the Bench We Share project because I had experienced grassroots peace work in action. It was as if I had 'come home' because, at last, I had made contact with a group of ordinary people who were tackling community peace building in the most difficult of circumstances. I felt at peace with myself because I was on the right track. I was inspired, encouraged and filled with a desire to support the Centre for Peace, Non-Violence and Human Rights and to get involved in the work. I had this burning desire to share my experience with as many people as possible.

As the first visit was made during a Sabbatical, I was able to share the experience with my local Sabbatical support group. The visit to Croatia dominated the meeting and it was as if all the other aspects of the Sabbatical were secondary. The chair of the group commented: 'Clive is talking continually about displacement of people, but it feels as if Clive himself is displaced.'

It was true that my heart was in Osijek, bound up with the individuals I had met and the issues they were seeking to resolve.

I kept thinking about the questions that had been asked of me by the Methodist Church. I felt angry and hurt by them, but they also challenged me to ask myself: 'Why should I be involved and why should the Methodist Church get involved?' With hindsight, I now believe it was a good point.

In response to the war, I learned there been protests in Serbia and in Croatia, and a flood of initiatives from Europe and beyond to bring relief, which included aid convoys of medical supplies, blankets and toys for children. There were also many peace organisations offering help, as well as conflict-resolution initiatives. Some of these efforts and initiatives had not always been that helpful in the long run.

So, I was grateful for the questions as they helped me clarify my own thinking and besides, I justified to myself I was responding to a request from the World Council of Churches to support work in reconciliation. However, I realised I was also responding to a deeper call to support and develop the work of healing the hurts of war. Over the next 28 years this call was to be put to the test many times.

I appeared before the committee on the last day of the Sabbatical, 29 April 1996, with the same enthusiasm and burning desire for the work of reconciliation.

The statement I received from the Methodist Church read:

Members of the panel were impressed by Clive's evident commitment and enthusiasm, his hands-on experience and his commitment to locality and practical out workings of his concerns. It was recognised that he brings a considerable range of skills and experience to bear on these issues and it was especially interesting to note his exploration of a multi-disciplinary approach to issues of conflict resolution which was thought to be an interesting and original contribution. The panel was, however, unclear how Clive's passion for Europe and his commitment to reconciliation and healing were necessarily connected, and the panel felt that more thought and work needed to be done on the relationship between these two. Members of the panel wish to affirm Clive in his exploration. They were grateful for the way that Clive wishes to dialogue with the Church as he seeks a way forward. The panel recommends that Clive be invited to return to the panel in a year's time.

I felt distanced by the committee and it felt as if it was saying: 'Calm down Clive, let the dust settle, get back into local church work and then review the situation.'

Dušanka Ilić
in 1996

Receiving the
Krunoslav-Sukić Award
for the Promotion of
Nonviolence,
Peacebuilding and
Human Rights by the
Centre for Peace,
Nonviolence and
Human Rights in
Osijek, Croatia in 2014

The May 2012 facilitators' workshop in Orahovica Country Park

Vlado with Snježana (left) and Nena, playing the fool at Barnes Close

Chapter 4

Initiation into the work

It was very difficult to settle down to normal church work. Coming back to work after a Sabbatical for any minister is difficult enough because the pace of a Sabbatical is gentle and slow. Then suddenly, when the Sabbatical is over, it is all go. Everyone wishes to talk with you and the phone never stops ringing. It's like returning to work after enjoying the silence of a retreat. Everything and everybody are very noisy in comparison. I found it rather difficult to return to the everyday problems of church life, preaching every Sunday and conducting baptisms, weddings and funerals.

Moreover, my eyes had been opened to all the effort being made by the Centre for Peace, Non-Violence and Human Rights and other groups to make peace happen in the region. I liken it to the experience of flying over an area from a distance of 30,000 feet. One sees the outlines of fields, houses, villages and towns, but as the plane descends you begin to pick out cars and even people. Once I was on the ground it all appeared confusing, but gradually I was able to see and hear more that would help me understand. By identifying with the boy offering the loaves and fishes to Jesus, I still had so much to learn.

My heart was very clearly in Osijek, yet I was living in Birmingham. I simply had to return to Osijek, so on 15 October 1996 I made a second, short visit to Osijek with my Anglican colleague, Revd Robert Johnson. He was the vicar appointed at St Michaels Anglican/Methodist Church. Robert, very laid back with a great sense of humour, was an ideal travelling companion.

One thing I needed to do was meet Dušanka again. The first visit had had such an overwhelming effect on me that I felt I needed to experience the situation in Osijek once more to clarify my feelings about what I had seen on that first visit.

The Sabbatical visit to Osijek had been financed by grants nationally and locally from the Methodist Church. I did not have the money to make another trip but, at the Methodist Synod meeting, I heard about a fund which was vastly under-used. It was out of this fund that the expenses for the next two trips were found. I have not had to use my own money for the work of Bench We Share or Touch of Hope. The money has always been there to cover expenses.

I was to learn more about the situation in Osijek and Baranja on this second visit by attending a Bench We Share workshop. This was in two parts and spread over three days, the first spent in Osijek. The second day in Baranja was to be spent with former Serb neighbours, sitting on the bench together. The third day would be back in Osijek, sharing with one another what it had been like to return to former villages and communities.

Because Baranja was under the control of UNTAES, residents of Baranja were unable to travel to Osijek. Dušanka needed special permission and an UNTAES escort to travel into the restricted area with former residents of the area. On the first day, Dušanka gathered together ten Croat participants who had been forced to leave their homes in Baranja. With great skill and empathy, she asked each participant how they felt about what had happened to them and how they had been forced to flee their homes with few possessions. She then explored their fears and expectations about meeting their former neighbours. Sadly, I was unable to join the group in Baranja as my time in Osijek was short.

This was my first experience of a group session. I noted the important features of the structure of the workshop to ensure that it was a safe space within which to work. At the start of the session, Dušanka asked the participants to consent to some basic ground rules to ensure that all participants would be able to take part. Listening to one another without interruption was agreed. Confidentiality was important to ensure that anything shared in the session would not be shared outside without permission of the person. To help bond the group, Dušanka used games which were fun and released the tension. Soft background music was played and she displayed pictures of positive images around the room, such as rural scenes of beautiful countryside. Everyone had a personal story of hurt and pain. The session became very emotional for everyone, including me. I remember one Croatian lady in tears as she described how she had lived in Bilje for years amongst her Serbian neighbours. Her 'friends', however, turned against her and started vilifying her for being a Croat to such an

Initiation into the work

extent that she feared for her life. She received death threats and threats to destroy her property. Reluctantly she decided to flee her house and seek sanctuary with relatives in Osijek. Anti-Croat feeling had become so bad that she ended up leaving under cover of darkness, clutching only essential belongings. I was touched that nobody minded I was present at such a moving event. I felt accepted as one of the group.

Baranja

Baranja had an air of mystery about it, the way people talked, but Robert and I were unable to go there. I wondered what it was like, so Robert and I decided to walk there from Osijek, along the main road which eventually leads to Hungary, passing through the villages of Bilje, Darda and the town Beli Manastir. The control-point was just outside Osijek, beyond which we were unable to go. People told me that the road would normally be very busy with trucks travelling through to Hungary. Robert and I found an empty, no-go area, an uncanny silence as we walked along the road. Hardly any cars passed us. We saw a huge cross which had been erected at the side of the road with flowers at its base. We stopped and read the names of people mentioned in the flower tributes; people who had been killed in the recent conflict. Their names were attached to the flowers and candles encased in red holders lying around. These candles were to be seen often along streets in both town and country. It is now common to see these candles, particularly at times of remembrance events such as around 20 November, the anniversary of the fall of Vukovar. It was an eerie feeling walking along this road. The air was still and there was no sound at all. In the distance we could see the checkpoint and at that point Robert suggested we turn back, which we did, heading back to the city centre. I wanted to continue to the checkpoint and talk with the soldiers, but Robert was insistent we head back to the city. The spire of St Peter and St Paul church loomed up over the houses and buildings of Osijek. As we turned around, I took a photograph of the empty road, a long narrow road which reminded me of Matthew 7: 13-14. *Enter through the narrow gate; for the gate is wide and the road is easy that leads to destruction, and there are many who take it. 14 For the gate is*

In spite of our differences

narrow and the road is hard that leads to life, and there are few who find it.

The road to peace is a narrow road, fraught with traps and dangers. God's peace is shalom, which is a Hebrew word meaning harmony, wholeness, completeness, welfare. It is something to be worked at, so I think of it in terms of peaceful behaviour. There can be no peace without justice. The road through Baranja had land mines on either side and there were signs reminding us of the danger from these mines.

In these few days, I became more acquainted with Dušanka, visiting her in her flat where I met her Serbian husband, Vlastimir. He was a retired colonel of the former JNA. Dušanka was born in Osijek. Her parents were born in Croatia, her mother being Croatian and her father Serbian. Her mother's parents were from Slovenia. She had three stepbrothers from her father's first marriage. She said that before the war she had a good family relationship with her brothers, but since she had stayed with her Serbian husband in Croatia, her brothers did not want to see Dušanka again in their houses.

She lived in the vast housing complex Sjenjak in the suburbs of Osijek. Sjenjak is a collection of 40 huge blocks of flats built between 1970 and 1988 and which have a curious numbering scheme. It was as if, after the blocks were built, numbers were assigned haphazardly, like somebody throwing up numbers into the air. Wherever the numbers landed on a block, so that block was assigned that number. Once I was lost and had to button-hole three sets of people, including a police officer, where to find a particular flat. Even the officer had no idea. Eventually, I found my way more by accident than design.

Before the war, Dušanka was working on a special project in schools, but the war interrupted that work. She continued to hold classes for children in the cellar of a block of flats in Sjenjak when the city was under siege from shells in 1991-1995. The children drew pictures on the cellar walls. One of them, a flower, is the cover picture of a book about Adam Curle (*Love in Danger* by Barbara Mitchels).

Vlastimir welcomed me to their fifth-floor flat. In a partition there was a pane of glass which had been broken after a grenade attack on the building and was not going to be replaced. Looking out of the window, I could hear and see trains which travelled through the estate. My favourite train was the direct train to Pécs in Hungary, a destination restored to the timetable after an absence of five years because of the conflict. For a short time, a direct train from Budapest to Sarajevo via Osijek trundled through Sjenjak back and forth once a day. The trains now rumbled on all day and through the night. I was struck by the fact that no safety concerns were ever expressed by parents of young children as there were no protective fences around the track.

Despite the war bringing much trauma and sadness to her and her family, Dušanka described herself as 'non-aligned'. She had gained much experience of mediating and supporting those who are being threatened with violence. After the outbreak of the war, she became involved with the Centre for Peace. She told me about an incident in which a Serbian mother and daughter, neighbours of her and her husband, were repeatedly intimidated by a Croat paramilitary group. They turned to Dušanka. Showing great courage, she was able to defuse the situation with the result that both mother and daughter still lived in the same apartment block, despite being pressurised to move away. Dušanka said that being involved with human rights work was very dangerous, but in spite of that, 'I am still here, I believe in people and they are essentially good. They need help to find themselves and find peace. I am a fisherwoman. I like fishing so much.' I can vouch for that, as Vlastimir and Dušanka loved to spend weekends at their country cottage on the Puškaš in Baranja, situated near the border with Hungary. They went fishing all day long and cooked their catch on an open fire.

Dušanka's assistant was Gordana. Over the years, Gordana has become a friend and an important link with Bench We Share. Excellent in English, she has two daughters who themselves speak good English. Gordana helped Dušanka with administration. She too lived in Sjenjak. She affirmed for me the importance of Bench We Share when she wrote:

To me the Bench We Share is the scent of quince in my grandmother's room. It is a silent, fluttering secret whispered in golden afternoon. And a gentle arm around my shoulder. It is a tear gleaming in the corner of my eye...To me the Bench We Share is the familiar fragrance of just made coffee. And endless talks not for children to hear. For the bench was our retreat too. Our loves and our sorrows were safe in its embrace.

Both Dušanka and Gordana told me that one of the important influences of the project was the book *Winnetou* by the German author Karl May (1842-1912). It is the story of a young Apache chief told by his white friend and blood brother Old Shatterhand, written in the context of the American Southwest. Winnetou is seen as a mediator who is able to bring together tribes who are in conflict with whites. However, he is killed and his death presages the death of his people.

The throw-away remark

At some point I suggested to Dušanka that she bring a group of Serbs and Croats over to Birmingham. My intention was for the group to have the space and time away from Croatia in a safe space, to engage together on how it is possible to rebuild trust and cooperation between the Serb and Croat communities in Osijek and Baranja.

I invited Dušanka to consider this invitation to visit the city of Birmingham and to experience the hospitality of the Methodist Church. The suggestion was in fact a throw-away remark I thought would never be taken up. I was proved wrong. Dušanka contacted me by fax to talk about it. This fax led to the first of many study visits to the UK and the start of a new, supportive network for Bench We Share and, subsequently, Touch of Hope.

We decided to bring two groups of participants to Birmingham. One group would consist of mainly Croats, who had to leave Baranja because of fears for their safety and property during the fighting and occupation of 1991-2. This group was now living in or near Osijek. The second group consisted of people, mainly Serbs, who stayed in Baranja during the occupation. The purpose of the visit to England was to provide a space for the two groups to meet, listen, hear one another and reflect together upon the question: 'How can we live together in peace and tolerance respecting our differences?'

Dušanka selected the participants according to ethnicity, age and gender. Most of the participants were involved in some way in local peace groups and were used to workshops.

Initiation into the work

In order to plan for the visit, Robert and I travelled again to Osijek in January 1997. The snow was deep and the conditions treacherous as it was minus ten degrees Centigrade. I was invited to meet a Quaker couple from England, Rosemary and Nick Street, who had felt called to rent a house in Beli Manastir. Nick and Rosie used the house as a base for meeting local residents from all nationalities. Rosemary offered English lessons and a listening ear to anyone who came to the house. Robert and I met Rosemary and Nick over a meal in a restaurant in Osijek.

They invited Robert and myself to stay with them for one night and return the next day with some of the participants from Baranja for the workshop. There was one problem. Robert and I did not have permission to enter the restricted area. Nick Street came up with a plan, whereby Robert and I had to conceal ourselves in their UK registered Land Rover. Nick and Rosemary knew the guards so well that they would not stop and search the vehicle. Robert and I travelled under blankets in the back of the land rover, feeling like illegal immigrants. I was worried that we would be caught. As we approached the control point, the land rover stopped briefly and Nick waved to the guards.

All was well and we were through the checkpoint. Robert and I dared not move until safe enough to utter a sigh of relief. Nick drove the land rover through little villages in Baranja in darkness. I occasionally glimpsed Serbian Cyrillic letters on shop signs, or the lights from cottages along the road. Landmines had been planted on either side, and signs warned us of the presence of the mines.

Eventually, we arrived in Beli Manastir where it was pitch-black and very cold. Rosemary and Nick made us very welcome, enjoying being together, but my memory of it was that it was freezing cold in the house. We slept well but awoke early to the sounds of barking dogs and cocks crowing. We had a simple breakfast of Kulen, cereal, fruit and vočni ĉaj (fruit tea). Early in the morning we set out on the road to Osijek to pick up the Serbian participants for the workshop, driving through thick snow. These participants had managed to stay in Baranja when it was occupied by the JNA (Yugoslav National Army). When we came to the checkpoint again, we were waved through as on the previous night. Robert and I let out a huge sigh of relief.

In spite of our differences

The Preparation Workshop

The workshop was held in the Students' Union at the University of Osijek. The participants were excited at the prospect of journeying together. It was a dream come true to visit England. However, they were also nervous. The 11 Serbian participants from Baranja were now meeting up with the seven Croat participants, some of whom had been expelled from Baranja and some had suffered at the hands of Serbs in Osijek. There were also four people of Hungarian nationality.

Some of the participants gave short biographies.

Ana, Croatian, 49 years, was born in Beli Manastir. Her husband was Macedonian and served as an officer in the JNA until 1991, when he had to leave Croatia. Their daughter Mia, 25 years, worked as an engineer. War separated their family. Ana writes:

My child has not seen her father for years, and I my husband for 5 years. We had contact by phone but through friends, because the telephone lines were cut. Then it became possible to go to Beli Manastir, so that I and my daughter went there every weekend, but he still could not come to Osijek. War brought us many calamities and destroyed our warm family corner and peace, but we are grateful to all those who had goodwill, love and understanding for our misfortune. Therefore, I WOULD LIKE TO SAY THANK YOU to those who sympathise with our misfortune.

Ana and Mia experienced pressure from armed men at night to move out of her flat. It was quite normal for paramilitaries to go to people with the intention of scaring them out of their houses.

Petar, 62, Serbian, a headmaster, spoke German with 30 years' experience as a teacher. I was challenged by his story of how he had to leave Bilje. When war broke out, he was on holiday at the coast but heard that his school had been evacuated, also to the coast, so Petar joined his staff and pupils. He made a film with the help of a TV crew about the children to show their parents back home. Petar jokingly called himself a 'war profiteer' because he had gained so much from the work of the Centre for Peace. He met Martin, a Croat who had also been displaced and they became good friends. They were two displaced people but from opposite sides. Petar was a very gifted person and a keen photographer. He organised many activities for displaced children including a course

Initiation into the work

in photography, compiling many photographic albums. He was also a great practical joker as I was to discover later. Petar's wife Marija worked as a bookkeeper. Their daughter J, aged 17, also came. She was in the fourth grade of grammar school.

Laszlo and Borbala were of Hungarian nationality. They lived in Osijek, but before the war they lived in Bilje, where they had their own house which they had to flee. Laszlo was a retired construction engineer and his wife Borbala a retired lawyer. They had two children and two grandchildren.

Katalin of Hungarian nationality, a Roman Catholic. was displaced from Baranja and lived in Osijek. Katalin worked as a mechanical draughtswoman in a private firm. She was engaged to Radomir before the war but decided not to get married because of the war, and because they were separated from their families.

Radomir was also a displaced person from Baranja, a Croat and Roman Catholic. Until the war he worked in the meat industry in Belje as a driver. He was now in the Croatian Army Reserve, mostly for financial reasons, because it was very difficult to find a job in Osijek. He was attending college in his spare time aiming to become a traffic planner. Their one desire was to return to Baranja and establish a home and family, living in peace with everyone living there and any who returned.

Martin Croat, born in 1943, teacher, active member of the Centre for Peace, Non-Violence and Human Rights in Osijek. His Serbian wife was born in 1945 and they had two sons and a granddaughter. Their oldest son had cerebral palsy. Before the war they lived in Bilje and after in the Settlement for Friendship for displaced persons at Čepin. Martin spoke German.

Stipan was born in 1952, in Šibenik and lived there until 1992 when he had to leave the town because of death threats to his family. He was married with three sons. He worked as a lawyer and assistant director in legal and personnel affairs. He also worked with the Association of Displaced and Exiled Serbs and with the Commission for Protection of Human Rights and Freedoms at the Democratic Forum of Baranja. He lived with his family in a two-bedroomed flat in Beli Manastir.

Katarina, Hungarian, born in 1955 in Draz and living in Kneževi Vinogradi where she worked in the primary school teaching Russian and German. She also worked at the Faculty of Philosophy in Novi Sad teaching English. Her daughter was 12 years old. She worked in the Centre for Peace and Human Rights in Darda and had participated in many workshops.

Gisela born 1973 in Osijek. Croatian, Catholic, a refugee from Baranja where she lived in a small village called Mece. She had a big beautiful family house there. 'I had to leave my home in Baranja during the horrible time of the war between Serbia and Croatia. I live now in Osijek.'

Marija born 1942 in Bosnia and Herzegovina. Croatian and Roman Catholic. 'I lived in Mece in Baranja with my husband and daughter. I had to leave Mece when war broke out and lived as a refugee in Osijek. The war has left deep pains in my soul but I say, thank God, the killing and destroying stopped. I try to forget the past; the present is bad and I must create the future.'

Suddenly, being faced with this large group in the Students' Union building was somewhat daunting. I sensed some nervousness in the group too as we helped ourselves to drinks and snacks. Dušanka had a lovely way of cajoling everyone and making them feel special, which helped defuse any tensions. Everybody was keen to say hello and ask each other about themselves. Communication was difficult for me as some struggled in English, but my German proved useful and we had fun trying to say what we wanted to say. I trusted Dušanka's professional way of leading the workshop and we lost no time in getting down to business. We began by introducing ourselves to one another. There was a particular poignancy about the start of this session which would lead to a journey to the UK. A huge step of faith for peace was being made. I thought of Abraham setting out on his journey of faith when he was called to leave his own country.

I was struck by how readily people wanted to participate in the opening exercise. Immediately, there was the buzz of people making contact, eager to start talking. It was a challenge to bring people back into the group and for each person to introduce the other.

My colleague Robert has a lovely sense of humour, and his account is full of witticisms as well as sharp observations on the significance of the exercise, as participants from opposing sides were sitting down together.

Initiation into the work

People were placed in pairs and asked to introduce their partner as themselves. Normally one might expect that this exercise would be presented in a light-hearted manner. These participants, however, were being asked to put themselves in the place of their former enemy. So, a Serb was being asked to say, 'I am a Croat, I was forced from my home and now live in a refugee camp' (and similarly with the rest of the group). This exercise was presented with great sensitivity knowing the traumas and suffering experienced by the members. Through this moving experience strong bonds were formed within the group.

This exercise is often used in our sessions because it encourages listening and empathy skills which are important components of healing hurts.

For Robert, the experience of being present in the workshop prepared him for working in an Inner-city parish in Birmingham. The parish had many refugees and asylum seekers who had fled war-torn countries. He was able to empathise with them and support them emotionally and practically.

I noted that Dušanka encouraged all participants to state their ethnicity in all the sessions she led. For the future workshops on the theme of identity, when participants were invited to state their ethnicity, whether or not somebody was able to say he or she is a Croat or Serb, became an important issue.

The prospect of the journey together united the group. Participants were asked to state their fears and anxieties about the visit to the UK. Robert and I did our best to allay any fears and anxieties. We spent a lot of time explaining the nature of the Methodist Church and the relationships between churches in Birmingham. Some participants were worried about where and with whom they would stay, or whether or not they would be accepted by the hosts. Some anxiety was expressed about travelling a long distance alongside a person who was from the other side.

The preparation workshop finished on a note of high expectations of a fruitful visit. However, some participants withdrew from the group because of the presence of people they did not like or because of atrocities that had taken place. Moreover, the Croatian government did not grant passports to some. With the

In spite of our differences

formation of the group complete, the necessary practical arrangements were made for travel.

It was full speed ahead to Birmingham.

Chapter 5

Birmingham

You, of little faith, why did you doubt? Matthew 14:31

In Matthew 14:22-32, there is the challenging story of Jesus walking on the water. The disciples were in a boat and the waves were being driven by the wind. The disciples were terrified, so Jesus goes out to them, reassuring them with the words, *'Take heart, it is I; do not be afraid.'* Peter answered him, *'Lord, if it is you, command me to come to you on the water.'* Peter got out of the boat, walked on the water and went towards Jesus. But when he saw the wind, he was afraid and, beginning to sink, he cried out *'Lord save me!'* Immediately, Jesus reached out his hand and caught him and said, *'You, of little faith, why did you doubt?'*

I was identifying with Peter. I had got out of the boat, been to Osijek three times and had thrown out the suggestion to Dušanka to bring a group to Birmingham. I was beginning to panic, self-doubt creeping in. Would the whole visit be a disaster? Would it help or hinder the process of reconciliation? There have been many times since when I have had self-doubt. I am constantly reminded of the words of Jesus to Peter: *'You, of little faith, why did you doubt?'*

With preparations complete in Croatia, it was time to prepare for the group's arrival in Birmingham. I had already organised a visit to the churches for a group of ministers from East Germany. This was a valuable learning experience for the forthcoming visit from Croatia. I marvelled at the readiness of Methodist churches in the area to welcome our guests from Croatia.

The former Yugoslavia was still very much in the news with reports of atrocities being committed in Srebrenica, Prijedor, Sarajevo and Mostar in Bosnia. Things were now becoming more intense in Kosovo, with the formation of the Kosovo Liberation Army, which led to increased oppression from the Serbian government. Vast numbers of people were escaping the fighting and fleeing to other countries in Europe and elsewhere.

I spoke about the visit around the area. I was relieved and delighted that the churches responded to the idea of welcoming a

In spite of our differences

mixed group from Croatia. Many people were keen to tell me of their holidays in Yugoslavia. They said how shocked they were to see the disintegration of such a country. Consequently, motivation was high among people to assist in any way. A GP, who offered to host, started to learn Croatian. I was anxious lest people would be resentful about the time it would take me to organise the trip, and how it might take me away from the normal work of a Minister. Churches throughout Solihull and Birmingham responded financially and in kind. The Barrow Cadbury Trust made a generous grant and very quickly we had raised £8,430.83 with the total cost of the trip coming to £8,392.10. Excess of income over expenditure was less than £40. Hosts came forward and a support group was formed to coordinate the visit.

We gathered a group of 24 Serbs and Croats, but in the end 23, plus Quaker Rosemary Street, came from 28 March until 7 April. Rosemary's presence was important because she was able to assist with follow-up work with the group on their return.

At the airport, the group appeared wearing badges showing a bench. We embraced one another and very quickly our guests were having their first glimpse of the English countryside. Travelling along the Solihull bypass, I was struck by the sight of hundreds of daffodils at the roadside, visible signs of spring. They reminded me of that famous poem by William Wordsworth:

When all at once I saw a crowd,
A host of golden daffodils,
Beside the lake, beneath the trees
Fluttering and dancing in the breeze.

Indeed, the daffodils were 'fluttering and dancing', such visible signs of spring, new life and resurrection, even if it was Good Friday. I was reminded of the words of 1 Peter 1:3 that *he has given us a new birth into a living hope through the resurrection of Jesus Christ from the dead*. We looked forward to Easter Sunday and to Pentecost, because the whole visit seemed to proceed with a fresh energy bringing people together within the group and in the churches. It reminded me of the disciples being filled with the Holy Spirit and being energised to work for peace. It was the start of something new and the group was the living hope.

Birmingham

What were we hoping to achieve in this visit? We were providing a safe space and time away from the war zone. We hoped all attendees would be able to experience healing and be re-invigorated to continue to work for peace in their own communities. It was important for people in the churches to know about the challenges the group faced in the aftermath of the conflict. We hoped we would learn from each other about building peace. We continually asked the question, "What can we learn from the war that will help us prevent destructive conflict in our own communities?" The prevention of conflict and war as addressed by Bench We Share became an important issue for the UK group. I hoped people would make connections between what had happened in the conflict and what happens in our own communities, particularly when there are racial tensions, riots or when community cohesion collapses. In these situations, fear and suspicion of the other are rife and there is a need to build trust and cooperation between different ethnic groups. The visit to Birmingham was not a case of us doing something for them, but rather that both sides were open to change.

Hospitality was provided by members of the churches. The hosts gathered at Acocks Green Methodist Church to greet their guests. With some nervous anticipation, they looked up as the travel weary group appeared at the doors and made their way inside. Door to door from Osijek, the journey had taken over 13 hours. Hosts had been asked beforehand if they spoke any foreign languages, in particular German, as many of the group spoke German. They also gave a short biography that had been reciprocated by their guests.

A small sum of money was given to each member of the group to supplement any money they might have. Matching guests to hosts took place quickly and it was left for Dušanka and me to return home. Each host family was given a little wooden bench, which became the trademark symbol of the project. The benches were made locally in Osijek and each bench was the same size but different in detail. The benches are still to be seen today in many homes and places of worship in the West Midlands.

Looking back at that first week, the programme was packed with varied activities that struck a balance between relaxation and opportunities for the group to mix together with hosts and in community. One host described having a guest as a life changing experience.

Dušanka, although a declared atheist, seemed very much at home in the churches we visited, which included a Roman Catholic Friary where we participated in the Easter Vigil. It was very much an inter-faith visit. Sikhs welcomed us to their Gurdwara, and Hindu worshippers into their Mandir. Although Dušanka found it difficult to understand faith, she nevertheless respected those who professed it and listened intently to people's experiences.

This was very evident when we visited Coventry Cathedral. The whole group was moved to tears as our guide explained how the old Cathedral, which dated back to medieval times, was bombed on the night of 14 November 1940 and left in ruins. That following morning, Provost Richard (Dick) Howard stood in the ruins of the Cathedral and with a piece of chalk wrote the words 'Father Forgive' on the sanctuary wall. These words are now used as the response in the Coventry Litany of Reconciliation. Two roof beams, which had been burnt, were found in the rubble of the Cathedral in the shape of a cross. These beams were pieced together and placed where the altar had been. Three medieval roof nails were formed into a cross and these became the original Cross of Nails. Six weeks later, Howard appealed for peace and reconciliation in a Christmas Day radio broadcast from the ruins of the Cathedral. To this day there are very strong links between Coventry and Dresden, other cities in Germany, and indeed throughout the world through the Community of the Cross of Nails.

Our visit to the Cathedral included a very moving film presentation of the story of the city of Coventry, including the bombing. The group emerged from the darkness of the small theatre with tears in their eyes. The bombing of Coventry brought back memories of the shelling and destruction of life and property back home. Members of the group also spoke of how Germany had occupied Yugoslavia in World War 2. A puppet state was set up in Croatia under the leadership of Ante Pavelić, who founded the Ustaša. Members of the Ustaša, the Croatian Revolutionary Movement, murdered thousands of Serbs, Jews and Roma during World War 2. At Jasenovac, an extermination camp was set up by

Birmingham

the Ustaša about 60 miles south of Zagreb. The ideology of the Ustaša was based on Nazi racial theory.

Out of the ruins of the old Cathedral, a new Cathedral was built in 1962, reminding us again of death and resurrection, the new arising out of the old. Martin in particular was moved by the inscription on the altar, Father Forgive. He reflected on the fact that the inscription did not say, 'Father forgive them', but just the words 'Father forgive'. No one person is innocent, we all stand in need of forgiveness.

The group was made very welcome at the Cathedral, but one thing surprised me. A member of staff could not understand why the group had been so upset when being shown around. I think it had been a long time since a group had been so moved by the Coventry story and the member of staff had underestimated the impact of the story on divided communities. The Cathedral became an important part of the programme on future visits from Croatia and Serbia.

We were given a civic reception by the Lord Mayor of Birmingham. The local Headteacher of Ninestiles School invited us all to an Indian restaurant for a lovely curry evening at the school's expense. How could we come to Birmingham and not visit an Indian restaurant? The Head of the school wrote a letter of appreciation for being allowed to be part of the experience by offering practical support. Churches, other community groups and schools worked together, united in their desire to be hospitable.

While in Milton Keynes, I had made links with the Community for Reconciliation (CfR) at Barnes Close, just outside Birmingham, where we spent the day enjoying the food and countryside. This gave the group the opportunity to share their war experiences and was the beginning of our long partnership with CfR. I warmed to Katarina who, together with Dušanka, led the session. Katarina shared how she defused ethnic tension in her school by using non-violent communication. In the way that she related to the teachers and children, Katarina was creating a culture of non-violence. Like the men and women chipping away at the Berlin Wall, she was chipping away at prejudice and discrimination in whatever form, against Croat and Serb. In fact, it was my first encounter with non-violent communication and I shall return to this later. Each member of the group shared experiences of the war and there was a lot of empathy shown to each other.

Public meeting.

A high point was the public meeting held at Lyndon Methodist Church on 1 April. Attended by over 200 people, members of the group told their own moving stories of being harassed and displaced. You could hear a pin drop as the audience listened so attentively to speakers such as Aleksa a Serb, who said, 'I can see a former member of the Croatian army in the meeting and I ask him please to come forward so I can shake his hand.' Radomir came forward and they shook hands and chatted briefly. Then, they embraced and Aleksa announced, 'We promise that we shall never fight each other.' He then called for forgiveness. 'My wish is that we forgive what was done in the war but not forget what has happened in these five years. For our future and the future of our children, let us work together for peace.'

This dramatic spontaneous gesture of reconciliation was a memorable moment in the whole visit and became a talking point in the churches for some time afterwards.

Katalin, married to Radomir, related her story. She explained how, until the war, she lived in Darda, Baranja and her fiancé lived nearby. The war started for her on 21 August 1991.

Our Serbian neighbours came out onto the street and started talking very quietly as if they expected something. The attack on the village started. At this time, I was with my best friends. I couldn't go home to see my mother because outside was shooting. In the evening the attack became more aggressive and to keep safe we went into our basement and we were joined by Serbs, Croats, Hungarians and Gypsies.

The worst thing was not knowing what was going on as it was quiet in the morning. But then it became frightening. People she knew were brandishing guns, wearing red bands round their arms and head.

We were scared and went back into the basement and then they started knocking on the door and after half an hour we let them inside. They started looking and searching for guns and

Birmingham

bombs. We knew these people but they pretended not to know us, their eyes were cold and callous.

As Katalin spoke, I could hear the sense of panic in her voice, worrying about her parents and not knowing where Radomir was. Someone aimed a shot at her. Miraculously it missed. That was the final straw and she decided to go home. Things went from bad to worse. When she arrived home, she was confronted again by Serbian neighbours wearing red bands and brandishing guns.

We were very scared and my brother and I and a friend decided to leave, taking a few things. One of the Serbian neighbours was very happy because I was leaving and he gave an ironic laugh and said, 'Aha, you run, you run.'

Leaving her parents, they went first to Bosnia and then to Osijek, where they eventually caught up with Radomir and his family. Life in Osijek was dangerous with continual shelling and she lost contact with her parents and brother. She finished her talk by asking the 'why' question.

In all this, I can't explain why our neighbours started shooting at us and why they killed so many innocent people and we have become 'the enemy'. Why have they robbed us and demolished our houses? We would like to come back to our house but it has been stripped of furniture, windows, door, bathroom and roof.

We little people have hope that we are strong and try to live together, but we know there are differences between us and the reason is the war.

Thank you for your work and I hope that one day we can welcome you into our home.

Telling the story was very important for the visitors and for an English audience. Many of the group remarked how cathartic it was to be able to tell their stories to people who had never heard them before. Many people had become weary in Croatia of hearing the same stories over and over again. Dušanka called all of us who were involved in the visit 'spontaneous mediators'. At every subsequent visit to the UK, there has been the opportunity to share stories with churches in open meetings.

This public meeting appeared to bond the group together, in spite of one challenging incident.

In spite of our differences

A group decision had been made beforehand not to talk about the causes of the war. This was something I had picked up from Dušanka. Discussions about who started the conflict are divisive and rarely productive. She insisted we should, instead, concentrate on being future focussed. However, one participant broke the rule, much to the anger of the rest of the group. The leader of the workshop commented that if that had happened at a meeting in Croatia, or Hungary, the workshop could have collapsed. Because the guests were so far from home, they had to hold in tension the differences between themselves. This appeared to strengthen the group and it became more cohesive afterwards. They were supportive of the rule-breaker. Although angry, they persuaded the person to look to the future and not concentrate on the past. I liken this to the work of mediators who encourage neighbours in a dispute to be future focussed in a mediation meeting instead of repeating, over and over again, what has gone on in the past.

The chief minister of the Birmingham Methodist District closed the meeting for us in prayer. She acknowledged the ways in which all of us contribute to the violence in the world and gave thanks for those who had shared their stories, because they had chosen the way of non-violence. She challenged us all to walk in the paths of forgiveness and peace.

The service of healing on 7 April, held at Acocks Green Methodist Church; included the Coventry Cathedral Litany of Reconciliation and the Laying on of Hands for healing. I felt it important that we all meet at the end of the visit in church to bring all our concerns, hopes and dreams before God alongside all the other activities. There was an open invitation for anyone to come to the altar rail to have hands laid upon them and receive a prayer for healing. Black and white, Croat, Hungarian and Serb all gathered at the rail to receive a blessing. Many said they experienced a sense of deep peace after the service. It was a truly ecumenical occasion to have Roman Catholic, Serbian Orthodox and Protestant men and women together in one place, acknowledging their need of God and finding comfort at the service and in one another. Prayer for Healing was to become an important part of our work.

Birmingham

What the visit achieved

One participant said:

We came as members of two groups, we go back as one group.

Something had happened in the group to bring them closer together. All participants had taken risks in deciding to come to England and the collective risk had fused them together. Some suggested the unity in the group would be short lived and superficial, but three things happened on their return to Croatia which suggests this was not the case.

First, Aleksa (who had embraced Radomir in the public meeting), was arrested at the airport and accused of armed outbreak against the Republic of Croatia. He was only released after his wife, who met the group at the airport, had contacted a lawyer. The fact that she had received a Pax Christi Peace award for her part in bringing two sides together in Baranja helped to bring about a speedy release. The incident reinforced the commitment of members of the group to support each other, irrespective of ethnicity.

Second, the husband of Milica, a Serb, committed suicide shortly after her return. The group were supportive of her as she struggled to look after her three daughters. Her husband had no previous history of depression but saw no hope in the situation improving for Serbs in Baranja. The death of her husband compounded her pain she had already experienced in her life. She regarded Croatia as her country and that of her parents, grandparents and great-grand parents. In one of our meetings, she recalled:

One morning in 1991, horrible graffiti appeared in my road. We will massacre Serbs, Serbs will hang. I work as a teacher in school and a new headmaster was appointed who suddenly said to me: 'you can't talk like this as a Serb in school but only in your house.' Then I asked myself, 'how do I speak differently today from yesterday?' And today I ask myself the same question.

With tears in her eyes, Milica spoke about the night when a Serbian neighbour's house was stoned. They were forced out of their home after receiving threatening and painful phone calls in the night. Scared stiff, they decided to move to Serbia taking their two children and one suitcase. They were joined by her sister and

In spite of our differences

family. But life in Serbia was very hard. They even had to collect wood from the frozen river to provide heat for the children. Milica went on to experience great family loss. As she prepared to return home from England, she still had concerns about her safety.

I am now going to see my house for the first time in six years and I took Croatian documents with me. But my house is just walls, nothing else and I have to decide what to do. I am scared. Guarantees about safety and obligations are just on paper. Should I go to Serbia? I don't have the money. Where? Where? Where? And now we have again evil phone calls. 'Go away Serbs, you didn't go yet. When we come...' Where do Serbs go?

And to finish, everything is hard, lose house, but to lose a dear person is hardest, because you can build a house but one can't create life.

After all these hard experiences, Milica writes that there is no hate in her heart. She does not know how to hate people, only war.

My father loved all people but not weapons.

Members of the group supported her after the death of her husband.

Lastly, the group helped Martin, displaced from Bilje in Baranja, to rebuild his house. It had been destroyed in the war and he had not seen it for six years. The house had been stripped of furniture, doors, heating, electrical and water installations. The situation at his parents' house was even worse – more damage and wood from the floors had been taken. He was thankful nobody had died in his family, but at the age of 55 it was hard to start again. At the time of the visit to England, Martin was living in Friendship Village, a camp for 2,000 displaced persons at Čepin just outside Osijek. He gave us his reflection on the whole visit.

What hurt me most in the war is the loss of trust between Croats and Serbs, friends and families. Ordinary people are damaged, who saw bad things but could not stop them happening. What did my wife Stojanka and I learn from our visit to England? Here in England, we feel free and accepted. We met many church communities in which we learn how the community can organise and experience many different activities, like singing and dancing, food, sports, parties that we don't have in our areas.

Birmingham

Martin expressed his hopes and desires for the future once he was back home in his restored house.

I want to set up a Centre for Peace, Peace House, in my village Bilje. There were people from both sides in this village. Soon Croats will come back to the village where there are now just Serbs.

With members of this group visiting Birmingham, we feel braver to talk with both nationalities in my village. We have planned this before but we have been scared. The big experience that I learned here is that I feel more confident to work with all nationalities in my capacity as leader in the camp for refugees.

The whole visit had been a tumultuous experience. My head was buzzing with everything that had happened and I knew I had to continue with this work. I knew too the experience of coming to the UK was important to the group and to the churches in Birmingham. This visit was to be the first of many groups to experience English hospitality, both in families and the churches.

Chapter 6

The first group visit to Osijek

There was considerable momentum for our visitors' hosts to make a return visit to Osijek. On 13 October 1997, seven of us returned to Osijek and Baranja for a week.

The participants who had been to Birmingham were eager to return hospitality and welcome us into their homes. We wanted to deepen the relationships in order to understand the culture, and how Yugoslavia had disintegrated. What did happen to 'destroy the harmony' in the Osijek area? In the words of Misha Glenny:

Relations between Serbs and Croats in Eastern Slavonia had traditionally been very good, even during the Ustaša regime. History indicated that it was most unlikely for vicious conflict to break out here. Something had happened to destroy the harmony in Eastern Slavonia.[10]

We were keen to see how peace was being made through Bench We Share and other peace groups. We looked forward to sharing our experiences with people back home so others could understand how peace is made.

Sharing food was a great start, bringing us all together. With the barriers down, eating in or outside people's homes strengthened the bond between us all. We visited the Kormoran restaurant, whose speciality is the extremely popular *Fiš Paprikaš* (fish paprikash). This is a traditional meal for Eastern Slavonia and consists of fish, usually carp, but also perch and catfish cooked in paprika sauce and served up with pasta and bread. The best is when the fish is caught fresh in the rivers and lakes and cooked over an open fire in a large cooking pot. I recall one occasion when we were outside, about to enjoy our meal, when Petar (a practical joker) kept on adding paprika and asking me to taste the sauce, watching keenly my reaction to the increasing heat. What he did not know was that I love spicy food, the spicier and hotter the better. Eating fish stew together outside becomes a great social occasion. The dish goes back to Austro-Hungarian times and is

---

[10] Misha Glenny *The fall of Yugoslavia* p107

The first group visit to Osijek

characteristic of dishes from communities living near the river Danube in that region.

The restaurant was situated in the lovely Kopački Rit national park, beyond the village of Bilje, which consists of 90 square miles of beautiful forest and water at the confluence of the Rivers Danube and Drava.

The beauty of the parkland was marred with reminders of the war, the many signs warning us of landmines. At that time there were thousands of mines. The task of de-mining progressed very slowly. In fact, on those early visits there were news reports of people being maimed or killed through stepping on land mines. I find that whenever I visit the region, I learn something new about the history or geography of the area. For me, this is an integral part of learning to live in a reconciling way.

When I first went to Baranja I was overwhelmed by people's hospitality. In one day, I was invited to four different homes and four dishes of fiš paprikaš at 12 noon, 2.30, 5 and 8 o'clock. When I told the second host I had already eaten some fish, she said: 'Well ours is much better than theirs.'

We lodged all with families, and three of the group stayed with guests they had hosted. Katarina had stayed with Margaret in Solihull, the start of a beautiful relationship and developing peace work of a new kind. Their friendship led exchange visits between young people in Birmingham and Solihull and their peers in Kneževi Vinogradi, Baranja. The young people from the Midlands ran playschemes for children from all nationalities. It pleased me greatly that the pairing of host and guest had gone so well. Guests were so pleased to welcome their hosts into their own homes and I was delighted church members wanted to see for themselves what the situation was like in Osijek and Baranja. Margaret described her interest in Bench We Share as being like:

A seedling struggling through an overgrown garden, which has become a plant whose shoots were fed and watered by Katarina and her family.

We were made welcome everywhere as we listened to painful stories concerning housing. Many families had been forced to leave their homes, some to refugee accommodation, others to cramped, inferior premises, or even damaged property. For various reasons

In spite of our differences

they were not yet able to return to their own houses and they may never do so. The government was not yet providing money to make damaged homes habitable, so there were many squatters. The situation was very complex. Politics and emotions ran high, but the work of reconciliation was going on and there were some returnees, albeit on a very small scale. Even when families could return, the feelings among neighbours, and sometimes family, did not allow re-patriation to a particular village. Under such circumstances, peace was very tenuous.

We were inspired by how Bench We Share was supporting people psychologically and practically, encouraging different nationalities to come together. One useful and important, practical addition to the work was the Bench We Share car, complete with the logo of the bench. I had many rides in this car to meet people and see peace building in action.

A good example of empowering local peace groups was the setting up of OAZA (OASIS)[11] which is still functioning in 2025. Dušanka invited us to meet with the members of the group. We sat in the small meeting room in Beli Manastir, the walls festooned with photographs of young and old attending events. The leaders jumped up and down with enthusiasm and were so delighted to welcome their first group from England. In nearly perfect English they told us how the group was formed and how they had been through the Alternative to Violence Programme, which teaches non-violent communication. The OAZA group was helping Serb, Croat, Hungarian and Roma to communicate in ways that connected with others to develop trust and cooperation. Once again, I was challenged by the group's commitment to creating peace in their local community. It was an example of ordinary people being empowered to make a difference by communicating in non-violent ways. The meeting was rounded off with generous helpings of local delicacies; kulen, cooked meats, pastries, juices, tea and coffee.

We visited the village of Popovac in Baranja where we met the local workers of the Bench We Share club. Once again, the leaders were delighted to welcome their first group from England. We

---

[11] Mirovna grupa OAZA Beli Manastir. Jozsefa Antala 3-31300 Beli Manastir oaza-bm.hr

The first group visit to Osijek

listened to the workers saying that although Serbian and Croatian children were together in school, after classes they separated, not wishing to play with each other. Unfortunately, relatives and parents sometimes encouraged these negative attitudes. The Bench We Share club gave them the opportunity to play and be together in their free time because in conjunction with the Osijek Centre for Peace, the children had been given a playground. As we were talking, we could hear children of all ages running round enjoying ball games and craft activities. The noise was deafening but as one worker pointed out, with tears in her eyes, the noise of happy children was infinitely preferable to the noise of guns. In the meantime, our waistlines expanded as we sampled the many cakes and dishes, another example of excellent hospitality.

We heard about the formation of the Lipa (Lime Tree) peace group, and how Bench We Share had succeeded in initiating and encouraging it. Members of this peace group were from different nationalities and religions. The group included people who had returned to their homes and those who had stayed during the conflict.

We wanted to know Dušanka's secret, how she had brought so many people together. At a very lively meeting we quizzed her on her methods. Dušanka introduced us to Mira, a Croatian woman from Popovac and a Serbian woman Dunja from Branjin Vrh. In her own inimitable way of speaking English, Dušanka translated the two women's experience of how they came together. The first step was for Mira and Dunja to be interviewed separately, then encouraged to meet together. There had been fierce fighting in the area and both women were traumatised by the loss of life and property. They were wary of having a joint meeting. Dušanka had listened intently to them both. Their relationships in the past had been good before the war. They decided to meet together on the 'little bench'. Dušanka prepared them both, using non-violent communication and encouraging empathy with one another. Dušanka told us how she had prepared others to meet up with people from the other side. Having had several joint meetings on the 'little bench', she invited each pair to sit on a 'big bench' and hold a bigger group meeting. The agenda for the group meetings was to answer the question: how is it possible to live in peace with one another in spite of our differences?

In spite of our differences

Mira and Dunja told us how they had been encouraged to run groups and train others, so there were always people available to give support. With smiles, they described how, at first, they were full of prejudice towards one another, which could have led to more conflict and violence. Through meeting together and Dušanka's mediation skills, they were able to communicate in a different way and build up trust. They both felt they were now contributing to rebuilding the shattered community and working with conflict constructively.

Talking with those involved with Bench We Share, we could see how the work had introduced a different way of being. By not using the language of blame, criticism or judgement, conflict was managed in constructive and creative ways. The imparting of skills and methods was important, such as in listening and responding. However, the main value of its activities lay in its ability to start the process of handling conflict in a different way. Through its work, participants were encouraged to believe in themselves and in each other's uniqueness. At the same time, it did not ignore the conflicts that existed between the different nationalities. People came from a variety of social, ethnic and educational backgrounds. What I loved about Dušanka's approach was that she was working with people at grass-roots level, people who were not in power or authority. They were often the poor and the poorly educated, who did not speak a foreign language. This was peacebuilding from below and it made a lasting impression on me.

Many people were not used to expressing their innermost feelings and thoughts to family members, let alone complete strangers in a meeting. Once this self-awareness process began, the participants experienced change, encouraged to express needs and feelings. This led to better communication in their relationships. Our presence and personal involvement were valued greatly. I appreciated Margaret's observation that 'their priorities will not be ours, necessarily, so we have to show patience and understanding.'

Sue had hosted Sara in Birmingham and did not know what to expect when she decided to go to Croatia, saying she could not have visualised the pain and suffering they had encountered. At first, she was a little nervous, but as the week went by she became more relaxed, forming a close bond with her host family, Sara and

The first group visit to Osijek

her two sons. Sue observed, 'the community may have escaped the shells, but it has torn their hearts and left them broken and scarred.'

Eager to travel into Baranja along the narrow road from Osijek, I was struck on the one hand by the landmine signs at the roadside and, on the other, by the emptiness of the road. I was reminded of Lincolnshire by the flatness of the countryside, the rural nature of the area. The lush green of the fields spoke to me of growth and new life, hope for the future.

Travelling to Vukovar, we passed ghastly reminders of the war. Gutted houses and buildings, homes once enjoyed by families of Croatia and Serb alike, places where children had played happily together. Such scenes were difficult for us, as a group, to see. Our hosts had prepared us for going to Vukovar. The description of its former days reminded me of Chester, a town of elegance, beauty and style. Nothing could have prepared us for what we now saw, war damaged houses and roads. We went to the Danube Hotel and sat outside drinking our coffee overlooking the peaceful river. There was something surreal about looking at the quiet flowing Danube on one side and the ruins of buildings on the other.

Amidst the destruction of Vukovar, the existence of a Youth Centre and Peace Centre were signs of hope. We appreciated the warm welcome given by the young people, some of whom were volunteers from Austria. In the midst of the sadness there was laughter with a commitment to seeking peaceful ways of resolving conflict. These young people inspired me to affirm what we were doing through Bench We Share and the link with Birmingham. They were so hospitable, offering us tea and biscuits, laughing as they practised their English and teaching us Croatian. They explained how they were bringing teenagers together from the different sides for sport and musical activities.

Having met Martin and his wife several times in England and Croatia, I was eager to see the camp for displaced persons in Čepin, just outside Osijek. I was moved by the visit. We saw rows of prefabs, children playing football, lovely allotment gardens full of vegetables to store for the cold winter. The greenhouse was stunning. All of this was a credit to Martin's hard work as a gardener. Martin was teaching others to grow vegetables and was a real support to displaced persons, so positive about life despite being displaced himself.

The camp was the terminus for the bus to Osijek at the end of the line. It was also the beginning of a new phase in the lives for so many people yearning to return to their original homes. We listened attentively to Martin's problems with his forthcoming return to Baranja. Later that week we were privileged to sit in his refurbished house, which was also the base for the Centre for Peace, Non-Violence and Human Rights in Bilje. Some of the work done on the house was the first piece of joint action by the group returning from Birmingham after Easter. Seeing Martin, his wife and his disabled son back in their home spoke to me of green shoots.

The group came back to Birmingham with a greater understanding of the work of Bench We Share. Members of the visiting group to Birmingham had given us a good idea of the situation in Osijek, Baranja and Vukovar. Now we had seen for ourselves and listened to people, which had confirmed the need for the work. We were also very encouraged by the community initiatives we had witnessed. We were determined to carry on inviting groups to England and supporting Bench We Share. Church members back home quizzed us about the trip as we shared our experiences and spread the good news of how peace was being made.

Price Charles – now King Charles III – with a translator
and Clive (above) and Katarina Kruhonja (below)
23 March 2016

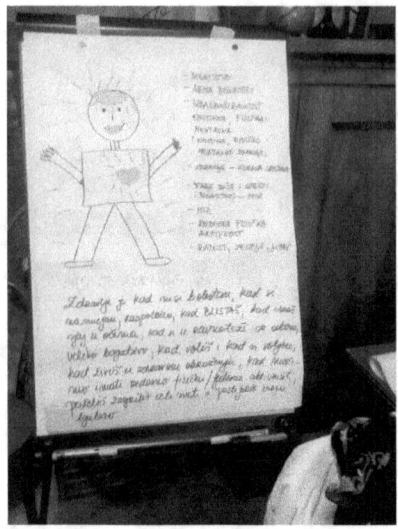

A flip chart from workshop session in Ilok
What does a Healthy person look like
February 2017

Nena and Judith up to their tricks
February 2017

Peace activist Dragica enjoying a joke at a workshop
October 2016

Chapter 7

On the move to Leamington Spa

How am I going to manage the ongoing work? This was the question going through my mind as we touched down in England.

The work of Bench We Share had taken a leap forward with the visit to Birmingham and there had been a successful return visit. I was now asking questions of myself, and others, as to how the work was to be managed, especially as I was due to leave Birmingham in August 1998. As the work grew, changes to its organisation were necessary.

A second, ten-day visit, was made to Birmingham on 4 July 1998. This visit had a different feel to it, which was to be expected because events in Croatia had moved on. The group was only 13 members, but mixed Serb and Croat along with some who described themselves as non-aligned. Whereas during the first visit Baranja was still under the control of UNTAES, the political situation had changed. The UN had left the area and the borders were open with the rest of Croatia. Displaced Croats were now returning to their homes and there were tensions between these returnees, and those who had stayed during the war, the remainees. Many homes were badly damaged or totally destroyed. Some were still occupied by Serb families. There was a great deal of economic distress with high levels of unemployment and a rising cost of living. Some firms were unable to pay their employees.

The visiting group of 11 women and one man represented four peace groups: the Centre for Peace, Non-Violence and Human Rights in Osijek, the Centre for Peace, Non-Violence and Human Rights Bilje, Oaza Peace group from Beli Manastir, and the Association for Peace and Human Rights in Baranja. This final group included a participant whose husband had come to Birmingham in 1997.

The main difference from the first visit to Birmingham was the inclusion of a 48-hour stay at the Community for Reconciliation

In spite of our differences

(CfR) at Barnes Close. The group regarded their stay at Barnes Close as the best thing that happened. The main activity was a simulation game. The beauty of such games is that they copy activities from real life, for the purposes of training and learning about oneself. One part of the group played a new civilisation – a nation with rules and customs. Others came to visit them in their homes. Group members realised how prejudiced and intolerant they could be if people did not conform to their way of life. Barnes Close has become an oasis of peace, a place of relaxation, laughter and playing, an essential part of the UK visits.

The visit also included a session at the Serbian Orthodox Church in Birmingham. One of my regrets about visiting the Serbian Orthodox Church on two occasions with groups, and also personally at other times, is that we could not build up a connection with the people who attended. On group visits, the presence of Croats was not welcome and as Dušanka had announced she was an atheist, she was rebuked by the priest as being a negative influence for peace. I naively thought we might be able to include the congregation in our programme. I was looking for possible interpreters as well. Despite several attempts to build up a relationship with the Serbian Orthodox Church over the years, nothing has come of it.

Five members of the group related their personal stories at the Methodist Church in front of a large audience. They were well prepared for this. The stories showed that in every war, including this one, little people suffer, because of somebody's great and sick ideas. One question, however made me cringe, which was asked by an elderly woman. She wanted to know if people had television in Croatia.

Dušanka was getting the hang of Methodist church life as she referred in her report to the 'obligatory tea and biscuits… served after the meeting.' The programme was not as full as before, so there was more time with hosts. Coventry Cathedral was again on the programme as well as a visit to inner-city Birmingham. This included a visit to a mosque. The composition of the group was mixed Serbian and Croatian and included some of those who stayed in the occupied part of Baranja and those who were forced to leave.

On the move to Leamington Spa

My desire to set up a mediation service for neighbour disputes was still uppermost in my mind. We visited United Neighbours, a similar service, based in Chelmsley Wood. We had a useful meeting, hearing about their work in preventing violence and how they viewed reconciliation. It was another example of how local people were being empowered to tackle conflict in their community. Conflict between neighbours was being transformed by learning to deal with it in creative ways. The visiting group was interested to hear about the local problems and think about how they could apply the techniques in their local situations.

Footprints

A small group had now been formed of people who supported the work. We needed a structure and a bank account. Following the success of the visits to the UK and Croatia, I proposed that the work come under Footprints, the resource network that had been started by three of us 1989. The original aim of Footprints: 'to build trust and cooperation between East and West', found new meaning in the wake of the disintegration of Yugoslavia. We had opened a bank account and it was decided to use this account for the burgeoning work.

At a meeting on 10 July 1998, the fledgling organising group for the work in Croatia decided on its first mission statement:

Encourage religious dialogue between Orthodox and Catholic churches and give emotional support for people traumatised by the war.

We were, initially, to work with Bench We Share.

I had come to the end of my time in Birmingham and some of the hosts who had been involved decided to carry on the peace work, albeit in a different form. This led to the formation of the Croatia Link, connecting young people from the churches to those in Kneževi Vinogradi, Baranja under the auspices of Katarina.

Leamington Spa

Journeying on as a Methodist minister to Leamington Spa was not easy as a family, as we had all been settled and very happy in Acocks Green. However, looking back, the timing was right for us and for the ongoing development of the work. As minister of

In spite of our differences

Radford Road URC/Methodist church I was grateful for its support and interest in the work since day one.

The move to Leamington Spa had a double significance because of the birth of Mediation and Community Support – a conflict support and mediation service for people who were experiencing disputes between neighbours. At the beginning of this book, I mentioned the verse from Ecclesiastes 3:1 *For everything there is a season, a time for every activity under heaven.*

Ever since my first contact with the Osijek Peace Centre and with Dušanka, I had been impressed with the role of mediation in peace building. I was determined to set up a mediation service locally. However, despite my best intentions to start one in Acocks Green, things just did not work out. The more I tried, the more the doors seemed to shut. However, soon after I arrived in my new appointment, a steering group was formed and eventually Mediation and Community Support (MACS) began.

Mediation and Parent Support (MAPS) in Wood End Coventry provided training and support for us. I did a mediation skills course with MAPS and began to take on cases and gain experience as a mediator. The course was led in part by Judith Halliday, who is now co-worker with me in the work in the work of Touch of Hope. Judith was one of two workers at MAPS and was successful in becoming our new worker for MACS.

Radford Road church was keen to host a group from Croatia and a third visit to England to the Leamington Spa Circuit was made from 25 June to 5 July 1999. The original intention was to have a mixed group of Catholic and Orthodox priests. However, it was not possible to bring together a group of Orthodox priests from Baranja because of the NATO bombing of Serbia. The conflict during the break-up of the former Yugoslavia had spread to Kosovo, with much bloodshed. Huge numbers of ethnic Albanians were forced to flee their country. Without UN authorisation, NATO led a three-week military campaign against the Serbs on 24 March with the objective of forcing the government to cease its campaign in Kosovo. The Serbian Orthodox priests did not feel it was right to come to the UK at the height of international tension. At the preliminary workshop in Osijek before the visit, we could see and hear NATO planes flying over Croatia on their mission to bomb Belgrade and Novi Sad in Serbia.

On the move to Leamington Spa

At first, it seemed a visit would not be possible, but a group of 13 eventually made the trip, representing the Orthodox, the Roman Catholic Church, Hungarian Reformed, Seventh Day Adventists and the Jewish faith. All but two were from Osijek and Baranja. The group consisted of the Executive Director of the Osijek Centre for Peace, lay people with two clergy, one each from the Catholic Church, Father Đjurica Pardon and Pastor Marijan Peršinović from the Seventh Day Adventist church. Both ministers had a big influence on the development of the work in Croatia and we owe much to them both.

Đjurica became somewhat of a celebrity as he spoke at the Birmingham Methodist Synod twice. There are not many people who can hold the attention of ministers and lay people for long in a Synod, but Đjurica did. He spoke very movingly about his own experience of the war and how important it was to support the project. Marijan came from Virje, Croatia and studied theology at Theological seminary in Maruševec, Croatia, gaining an MA in leadership at Newbold College in England. He became a Seventh Day Adventist pastor in 1993 and, while pastor in Beli Manastir, Dušanka invited him in 1999 to be a participant at workshops in her project Bench We Share. The workshops were for religious leaders and teachers from Baranja and Osijek region. Marijan was active as a participant in that project from 1999-2000.

Two preparation workshops were held in Croatia, the first of which involved me and a colleague.

The programme followed a similar pattern to the second visit. From the preliminary evaluations, the group said Coventry Cathedral and the time spent together at Barnes Close were the most significant for them. At Coventry Cathedral, half the group was overcome with emotion after watching an audio-visual presentation of the destruction of Coventry. The mood of the group and momentum of the visit changed and this prepared the ground for the time at Barnes Close, when the group was able to share at a deeper level, articulating fears and anxieties. The sessions focused on issues of health and healing. The aim was to encourage the expression of feelings to answer the question: What makes for health and healing within our own communities? The workshop ended with the laying of hands for healing.

In spite of our differences

Andrijana Sili

At the open public event at Radford Road church, Andrijana, a young Croatian school teacher from Osijek, shared her inner journey. She spoke to a hushed audience about how Serbian forces had attacked her village, Sotin, destroying property and taking away non-Serbs. She held up a little piece of concrete and told us that this was all she had left from her demolished house. Andrijana spoke about how she loved her father. He had always taught her to treat others in caring ways and to respect everyone. Her father had been cruelly taken away from her and there was a wall of silence as to his whereabouts. 'I just want to know the truth about what happened to my father,' she said to the many tearful people listening. The horror of the war had made a deep impression upon the listeners. Afterwards, we sat quietly to reflect upon what we had heard.

Andrijana had to wait many years to hear the truth about her father. For a long time in Sotin there was a tent with the names and pictures of people still missing, including her father. Over the tent were the words *Hoćemo Istin* which translates as 'we want the truth'. A simple memorial has now replaced the tent, displaying the names of those who had died or are still missing.

Eighteen years later, in 2017, the Balkan Transitional Justice newsletter published an article about what had happened in Sotin. An investigation was launched by a son whose father had been taken from his home and shot by Serb forces. A mass grave with 13 bodies was found and exhumations took place. A trial followed, leading to the sentencing of two members of the local Serb-led Territorial Defence Force. Searching for the truth was left to the families of the victims. I met with Andrijana for a Q&A session:

What were your reasons for joining Bench We Share workshops? What were you hoping for?

My colleague and I worked together at the same school. One day she mentioned Bench We Share and I said to her that the activities sound interesting and I would like to join them. When I first went to the workshop, I got the insight into the project and I realised I had to tell my side. It was difficult but I never gave up. That was my first exploration of feelings about which we did not talk at home. We all had the wounds we bore and lived with them

On the move to Leamington Spa

but nobody spoke about their feelings. We knew how we felt, but we did not talk about our feelings because it was too painful. Now for the first time ever, I was talking publicly about my biggest wounds.

I remember not calling my family for a long time and when I did eventually call, I cried buckets. My brother was very worried as I was crying so much. But when I spoke about the activities of the Bench We Share, it was a catalyst for also my brother and mother to share their feelings. At the time it was painful and difficult, but in the end, it was healthy for us all to share how we felt.

Do you have any news about what happened to your father?

Some of my dad's bones were found in a mass grave.

He was killed near the village on 26 December 1991. When the peaceful reintegration started, his killers knew they would be discovered. His body, with 13 other bodies, were thrown into a cave with animal bones in a village slaughterhouse. This crime was discovered in 2013 and my dad was buried in that year.

Thinking of the word 'justice', what would you like to happen to the people involved in the disappearance of your father?

The man who killed my dad was his friend. That's what my dad thought. My dad cannot be brought back. I do not think about punishment. I do not think about that man.

How do you feel towards your dad's attackers now?

I cannot generalise. I've never considered that. There are good people and bad people. I hope justice will be met. But I'm not burdened with it.

What does the word 'reconciliation' mean to you?

Reconciliation is the desire of both sides for trust and coexistence. I do not have the desire to trust the person who killed my dad.

Do you go back now to Sotin?

In the centre of Sotin is a monument to all the victims of Sotin and to my dad. I go to Sotin to light a candle in those places. In Sotin I have friends and a godparent whom I see. I go to Sotin four or five times a year.

In spite of our differences

Talking with Andrijana made me realise all the more how many people in the region still live with pain and unresolved issues of justice. For some people like Andrijana, the journey to reconciliation continues to be painful and hard. For some years she had wondered how her father had died. Now that she knows, the truth brought sadness and hurt.

Community for Reconciliation

The organising group now had to face the question of whether to seek charitable status or work with an existing charity. I had already made contact with Community for Reconciliation (CfR). The Charity Commission recommended we find a charity with similar aims to work with. We applied to the trustees of CfR to become part of their work and after some time we received the news that we would be able to use the charitable status of CfR. The charity stipulated that we had to organise all our own fundraising and we could not rely on CfR for funds. However, CfR was happy to publicise our work. Since the merger, the work has benefitted financially. We became known as CfR Footprints and a bank account was set up in our name. The director of CfR, Rev John Johansen-Berg, chaired the first inaugural meeting on 15 November 1999 at Barnes Close.

The first meeting of CfR Footprints took place three days after I received the news that I was to be awarded an MA degree in Peace Studies from Bradford University. I noted in my diary that 12 November was Results Day and it was with much trepidation that I rang the Peace Studies department to see if I had passed.

A fourth visit to Leamington was arranged for the end of June 2000, with 11 participants plus Dušanka, three men and eight women. Five were from Osijek and the rest from Baranja. The group included our first visitor from Bosnia, a Muslim woman living in Beli Manastir.

As well as the programme having a community focus, a new activity was a visit to the Department of Peace Studies at Coventry University with Professor Andrew Rigby and Dr Carol Rank. I felt it was important we had a link with Coventry University. I hoped a student might wish to become involved with the programme and thus we would benefit from some current academic thinking about the role of non-governmental projects in peacebuilding. Sadly, this never happened.

We had a non-verbal 'communicating through art workshop' in which the group had to draw a picture of a healthy community without talking to one another. For one participant Suzana, who had studied psychology at university, this workshop was very special because of what she learned about herself and other members of the group. She said she had moved on in her own journey of self-discovery and faith. 'The workshops helped me to restore my faith in God and in people.'

Time was also spent at Barnes Close.

The Cross of Nails

The climax of the visit was receiving a Cross of Nails on the 9 July at Coventry Cathedral. We became a member of The Community of the Cross of Nails, a world-wide network of churches, charities, peace-building centres and educational and training organisations all of which are inspired by the Coventry story of destruction, rebuilding and renewal. Dušanka received one Cross and I received a second at a very moving service. The first Cross now resides in the Centre for Peace, Non-Violence and Human Rights in Osijek. The second is currently in Nuneaton Methodist Church. Despite describing herself as an atheist, Dušanka was delighted that the work of Bench We Share was recognised in this way. The Coventry story continues to inspire groups from Croatia, Serbia and Bosnia and Herzegovina.

Below are some of the reactions to the workshop in 2000 from their evaluations.

I think I am one step closer to purify my soul from war traumas, which I don't like to talk about and I never do that. I just don't have words for that. I am filled with sadness because here in England there are people who are willing to listen to me and to help me.

I had various feelings, fear, insecurity, but I felt better and better, my hosts were wonderful.

I found myself again.

When I heard we would have healing hurts workshops I was afraid how I would react. But when I went to Barnes Close it was

In spite of our differences

better. I did not know there was so much pain in me. My mask began to fall as I was standing in the middle of Coventry ruins. I am an atheist but that place has a soul not only for those who believe in God, but also for everyone who felt the suffering pain. There I started to cry for the first time, because I felt very strong faith that human beings can do anything that he wants only if he believes in himself. Barnes Close was hard and painful. For the first time I was able to say aloud my sorrows. I have that strength from my host's love and unconditional support. The workshop changed my life forever. People that I did not know they even exist made me feel that I am worthy, they released me from guilt, helplessness and uselessness.

Chapter 8

From Bench We Share to Touch of Hope

Conflict had developed in the Footprints committee as we disagreed over strategy. It was now five years since my initial visit to Osijek and there had been group visits to and from England. Questions were being asked by committee members about the purpose of the UK visits. Concerns were expressed about the financing of such visits and some people were saying we should be supporting the work in Croatia financially, not be bringing people to the UK. The money spent on bringing the groups to the UK could be spent on work in Croatia. This argument has been used continually over the years. Taking the long view, our observation has been that participants are more likely to stay with the work and train as facilitators if they have been to the UK. I did not know this at the time because it was to be another 12 years before we began to train facilitators. I felt intuitively that there was a value in offering impartial hospitality to groups visiting the UK. People who had come to the UK valued staying with an English family as an invaluable insight into English family life. Moreover, many prejudices had been removed, including those about the English being cold, stingy and hostile. Many visiting guests established very strong friendships with their hosts. Others felt we should be concentrating on training trainers. This too has been a constant refrain since the beginning of the programme. The reality was that the content of the group meetings was evolving. At this stage of the work, we did not know how the programme would work. We were working very much in the dark, and it would be some time later that we would begin to equip facilitators to lead group sessions in their own communities.

Moreover, there had been organisational difficulties with Bench We Share workshops when groups arrived from England. This led to frustration and discontent among the UK visitors. The numbers of people turning up to the sessions was far fewer than those who said they would come. I felt very torn, as on the one hand there was criticism of Dušanka, but on the other hand I could see Dušanka was under strain and her health suffering. While some of the criticism appeared justified, because I could see that it was very frustrating to turn up to workshops with falling numbers, I felt the criticisms were insensitive to the fact that Dušanka herself had experienced suffering to an extent unknown to those in the UK. Furthermore, we did not understand fully the pressures Dušanka and potential participants were under. I felt very uncomfortable being in the middle.

Things were also moving on in Croatia. Bench We Share's role was to open up communication between different sides of the conflict. A pattern of workshops was emerging, dealing with health and healing, but we needed more workshops dealing with the many issues people faced in the region. That was one point that we all agreed on. When participants came to the UK and shared their stories, the pain of what had happened in the war was laid bare before us. We needed to think very carefully about our key themes. Moreover, the UK group that had visited Vukovar was deeply moved by the visit, so we were aware of the need for healing the deep hurts. I remember Katarina Kruhonja saying to me that we cannot expect healing to happen just after a few meetings. There were no quick fixes. I felt that because the needs were so great, any programme organised by CfR Footprints had to address those needs.

The situation in Osijek, Baranja and Vukovar was changing because more people were returning to their former homes and beginning to settle back into their communities. The Centre for Peace and other groups were very active in working for reconciliation in the area. I felt it was important to work alongside the groups in Croatia, to be a resource for those working for peace in the region. I acknowledged Dušanka's unique contribution in setting up Bench We Share and her commitment to peace.

There were a number of factors that led to a consultation being held at Coventry Cathedral from the 1-5 October, bringing together six people from Croatia; Katarina Kruhonja, president of the Centre for Peace Osijek and two other representatives of the Centre for Peace; two participants who had visited the UK, Father Đjurica Pardon a Roman Catholic priest in Batina, Baranja and Pastor Marijan Peršinović, together with Dušanka.

From Bench We Share to Touch of Hope

Alongside the visitors from Croatia were representatives from Coventry University. The reading I had done for the MA in Peace Studies had alerted me to critiques of so-called 'second track intervention' in the former Yugoslavia. Official diplomacy and summit politics belonged to first track and the role of Bench We Share was an example of second track intervention. International agreements like the Dayton Peace accord in 1995, belonged to one level of intervention – peace from above. Bench We Share's work was ensuring local people can live together with no violence – peace from below.

I felt it was important that we learn from the insights of academic research. I recalled the remarks of the Europe secretary in the Methodist Church six years before, when he challenged me about why I should be involved in the work of reconciliation. When does intervention become just interference in another country's internal affairs? Groups on all sides in Eastern Slavonia were working together on solutions at a very early stage and were continuing to work together after re-integration. What more could we do from the UK to add to what was going on locally after re-integration? One of my concerns about the UK study visit was that it would encourage people to leave the region and come to the UK, not staying in their own country and working for the rebuilding of their communities.

Barbara Mitchells, a PhD research student at Bradford University Peace Studies department, facilitated the consultation. It was recognised that four initiatives had come out of Bench We Share. These were the Croatia Link, merging our work with Community for Reconciliation, aid to Sotin kindergarten and the formation of Bilje Peace Centre.

The Croatia Link started after I left Birmingham to be the minister in Leamington Spa. Hosts from the 1997 and 1998 visits continued to meet, wanting to maintain links with friends in Croatia. They decided to focus their attention on the needs of young people in Baranja. In 2000, a group of 12 young people, plus four leaders, stayed with host families in the Birmingham/Solihull area, visiting Oxford, Stratford and Coventry Cathedral where the reconciliation work made a deep impression on them. They had time together in a residential centre. The following year, four of the young English hosts and two adult leaders spent five days in

In spite of our differences

Baranja. They had a moving visit to Vukovar. These two visits were so successful there was a strong desire to continue. The link was still going strong 20 years later.

Andrijana Sili, who came to Leamington, was the contact person for the Kindergarten in Sotin. Philip, a committee member, was keen on supporting the Kindergarten with equipment and toys. It was a real delight to be able to present the group with donations of money and toys. I was a little nervous about this gesture as I was always at pains to point out that Bench We Share is not an aid project, as there were plenty of aid projects around but very few programmes concentrating on bringing people together who were in conflict.

Merging our work with the Community for Reconciliation had been an important step forward. We were now connected to a body of supporters who were committed to reconciliation. We had a centre to which we could invite people to stay. We were in touch with other groups around the world who were working for reconciliation.

After the return from England, participants in the first group established a peace group in Bilje Baranja, while it was still under UNTAES control.

At the consultation, the following objectives for a new project were decided upon: to develop the awareness of wounds and hurts on a personal, community, town and national level and to raise awareness of the importance of healing. The promotion of good health of the participants was important. To achieve this, we felt it was important to give space and time for people to open up, to provide an accepting climate to allow people to acknowledge their own and each other's hurts, without judgement and in an atmosphere that encouraged growth.

Considerable discussion took place about the name of the project. We decided Touch of Hope, which translated into Croatian is Dodir Nade. In some Bench We Share workshops I had offered prayer for healing and this had become an important part of the workshop programme, so much so that the members of the consultation group wanted to reflect the prayer for healing in the title of the project. Consequently, the word 'touch', meaning the touch through the laying on of hands combined with the word 'hope' became Touch of Hope or Dodir Nade.

From Bench We Share to Touch of Hope

I remember being asked by Marijan to lead healing prayers in a community centre. The group met in Vukovar, a dozen men and women who looked very sad, gloomy and depressed. I did not know any of them and would not see any of them again. It was a difficult situation going into an unknown group, while not knowing what they expected. Marijan had told them I could offer prayer for healing. I said some prayers and gave a short reflection and laid hands on each member of the group. After the prayers, it was remarkable how the atmosphere changed from being dark and gloomy to light and almost cheerful. People smiled, laughed, as if a dark cloud had been lifted. I was reminded of what Adam Curle had written about the Black Cloud in his book *The Fragile Voice of Love*:

Essentially, it is like a nasty smell. It's there. We are unpleasantly aware of it, but we get accustomed to it. It can be defined as a kind of universal emanation of unhappiness, misery even, frustration, sense of loss. It is the impact of the accumulated misery, despair, desperation forged by the century-long slaughter since the outbreak of World War 2, a butchery unparalleled in human history. It is, I am sure, responsible not only for immeasurable grief, but for desperate, foolish and immensely cruel actions.[12]

Clearly the prayer for healing had an important part to play in the healing process.

The word hope had been chosen because the work so far had given participants a new lease of life and brought back a sense of purpose to their lives. Hope had been communicated through the love and care of one another. This did not mean that issues and problems disappeared, but participants felt able to cope more effectively. Rebecca Solnit writes:

Hope does not deny realities rather it means facing them and addressing them. Hope is not the belief that everything will be fine. It is about broad perspectives with specific possibilities, ones that invite or demand that we act. Hope is an embrace of the unknown and the unknowable, an alternative to optimists and pessimists.[13]

---

[12] *The Fragile Voice of Love* Adam Curle p8
[13] *Hope in the Dark* Rebecca Solnit page x

In spite of our differences

She quotes the theologian Walter Brueggeman: *memory produces hope in the same way that amnesia produces despair, grounds for hope lie in the past.* To illustrate this, older group members remember when people of all nationalities lived and worked so well together in Vukovar and Baranja. *We lived well together and we shall live well together because we did so in the past.*

Dodir Nade

We decided that our mission is to motivate, empower and help men and women wounded in war through the process of healing.

Motivate

Choosing the word 'motivate' reflects its synonyms – drive, inspire, prompt, move, stimulate, encourage. I recall my experiences of being a minister in working with the bereaved, having conducted hundreds of funerals. I am also aware of people coping with the loss of a pet, a job, part of the body or experiencing a divorce. The loss saps both physical and emotional energy. Dodir Nade participants have sometimes experienced extreme loss of loved ones, property, relationships, employment, identity, experiencing a great deal of pain. I am not surprised when people cannot even contemplate joining the programme. Consequently, motivating men and women to come on a workshop is a challenge in itself, a question of people believing things can be different, people can move on after their devastating experience of war.

Empower

It is important that each person is empowered to create their own answers to situations. Participants often complain of being powerless to change their situation, or talk about the time when they were forced to leave their homes, powerless to resist. Empowerment is about equipping participants to be able to challenge discrimination and work with conflict in constructive ways. It is linked with the ownership of a situation. Responses, beliefs and actions remain with the person. This is about taking responsibility for one's actions and becoming part of the solution as well as being part of the problem. An inspiring example of taking ownership, as I described earlier, is that of Katarina

Kruhonja, working with others in setting up the Centre for Peace, Non-Violence and Human Rights in Osijek.

Men and women

All people, irrespective of nationality, creed, religion or no Faith.

Process of Healing

Looking the word up in the dictionary, process is defined as 'a systematic series of actions directed to some end or a continuous action, operation or series of changes taking place in a definite manner.'

We acknowledge that healing the hurts of war is an ongoing process that may take years, during which a person will take one step forward and two back. A lot depends on an individual's own motivation and willingness to engage with the issues affecting them.

At the consultation, we decided our goal as a programme was 'to build a healthy society, based on a culture of non-violence in war torn areas of Eastern Croatia.'

It was agreed to hold a series of six group meetings for each programme cycle. The themes of these meetings would be Health and Healing, Communication Skills, Identity, Wounds, Forgiveness and Reconciliation. We have stayed with these themes, which we call our basic training. In more recent times we have added other themes. The group sessions were to be held over a weekend, apart from the two sessions on Communication Skills and Identity. Visits to the UK would continue where practicable, but participants had to complete the basic training first. The sessions were to be led partly by local leadership, and partly by me with the assistance of another leader from the UK.

When we made the transition from the Bench We Share to Dodir Nade, Dušanka helped us for a while in an advisory role. We continued to meet up when I was in Osijek and she was always very encouraging. Sadly, she became ill and her mental health deteriorated to the extent that it became difficult to communicate with her. She became a shadow of her former self. It upset me to think she was no longer the person she had been when she led workshops in such a dynamic way. In 2016, I received the very sad

In spite of our differences

news that Dušanka had died. Her funeral was arranged very quickly and so I was unable to attend. Because of the way she had welcomed and influenced me in 1996, this book is dedicated to her.

Chapter 9

Introduction to the workshops

Whenever I give talks about the work of Dodir Nade, someone will invariably ask me:
So, what happens on a workshop?

My mother could never get her head round the word 'workshop'. Looking up the word in a dictionary, it can either mean 'a room or building in which goods are manufactured or repaired, or a meeting at which a group of people engage in intensive discussion and activity on a particular subject.' My mother could only think of the first meaning of the word. Whereas the second meaning is a more accurate description of what happens on a Dodir Nade workshop.

Building on what I had learned from Dušanka about running a group session, we have to ensure each session in the programme is an emotionally safe place to meet. Of course, we can never guarantee that a session is 100% emotionally safe because we never know how participants will react emotionally. But we do everything possible to make it a safe place in which to work. To this end, we agree the rules of the session (*pravila radionice*). My co-workers and I ensure that we agree to listen to each other, that we respect one another, that we agree to talk from our own experience, which is known as 'I speech' for short, (*ja govor*). Each of the participants has the right to pass. This means that if a person does not want to take part in an activity, then that is fine. Confidentiality is also important. One rule, which always makes me smile, is one on which we all agree; to be punctual. I can count on one hand the number of times when everyone has been on time. We all agree to switch off mobile phones or to put them on silent, but inevitably in the middle of a highly emotional exercise somebody's phone will sound.

So, faced with a new group of people, including some who may not know anyone else, it is important to establish a way of working which will ensure a positive experience for all participants. We ensure that people know what the topics are, and what the hours of work will be (*plan rada*). Games (*igre*) are important and serve an important function, particularly when the energy level is low, for example after lunch or when there has been some deep emotional sharing. At the beginning of a programme, getting to know each other's names is often best done in a game.

We ask for a commitment to the whole programme of sessions. In the early days of the work there were more participants who dropped out of sessions than now. There are always people who fall ill or who have a family crisis, and they tend to miss sessions. However, in recent times the fall-out rate has dropped, which I believe is the result of better management of the sessions and follow-up.

Eating together as one group is very special. We always ensure that wherever we are staying we eat well. A former President of the Methodist Church, Rev Inderjit Bhogal, who was brought up as a Sikh, spoke publicly about how the community kitchen, the langar, is an integral part of Sikhism. I remember him using the expression 'first we eat, then we meet.' On the workshops, it is in the dining room over a tasty meal that we can talk, laugh and enjoy being together as a group. Whatever has happened in the sessions, when we come for a meal, barriers are down. All are equal, whoever we are, wherever we are from. We meet one another as human beings. For a Christian, that reminds us of the central act of worship in the Church, the sacrament of Holy Communion in which bread is eaten and wine drunk. We think of that meal as being a 'foretaste of the heavenly banquet'. Having crossed the threshold onto the meetings, eating as a group unites us and helps to dispel fears and anxieties. It brings hope, just as Holy Communion points to the future feast of the Kingdom of God.

We aim to have at least three leaders for each workshop. Snježana Kovačević is our current local worker and has long been associated with Bench We Share and Dodir Nade. She left us for a while but to our delight and relief, she has returned. Snježana was born in 1973 in Osijek, studied theology at the Evangelical Faculty in Osijek and, since 1996, has worked with the Centre for Peace in Osijek with exiles, refugees, wounded people and victims of the war. She has gained a lot of experience working with different groups of people. She also worked with the international peace

Introduction to the workshops

organisation Pax Christi International. She is currently self-employed, helping groups and organisations to apply for EU grants.

Nena Arvaj has just stepped down from being our worker and has a long association with our work. She was born in Vukovar and she too studied at the Osijek Evangelical Faculty. She is very experienced in leading workshops and working with all ages. For some time, she lived in the divided town of Mostar and worked with the Christian organisation Novi Most (New Bridge), which works on both sides of the bridge destroyed in the war. She has travelled far and wide in the region including to Albania, working with groups on issues of non-violence. Snježana and Nena spent a lot of time together as teenagers in Orahovica. Snježana and Nena are indispensable as they organise groups, support participants, look after the practical arrangements and, most important of all, translation of materials and interpreting at workshops.

One of the many strengths of Touch of Hope is the way in which we draw on different disciplines. Judith Halliday, my co-leader from the UK, brings a wealth of experience and expertise in training in conflict resolution and working with families. As the coordinator of Mediation and Community Support, she has had years of working with conflict in creative and constructive ways. She also brings to the work her experience of living in South Africa under Apartheid, an experience of cross-cultural working in unjust environments. When Judith and I are not there, the sessions are taken by the local team.

Occasionally we hold 'taster workshops' which last one day. They give participants a flavour of what to expect on a full workshop, as some people are nervous about committing themselves.

Chapter 10

Healthy communication, the jackal and giraffe

There are ten people in the group. To protect their identity, their names have been changed. I hope they will give you an insight into how the workshops work, and their impact upon the group.

Amina knew from day one of the sessions that she was going to find Aleksandra difficult. There was something about her which annoyed her. Amina did not let her feelings be known about Aleksandra in the first session. She was too polite to say anything and besides, everyone was on their best behaviour. Amina was partly dreading the second session because she did not want to make a scene or a fool of herself. She had arrived in Osijek at the Bible college exhausted, having travelled from Sarajevo in Bosnia and Herzegovina, the furthest distance any participant has had to travel. In the first session Amina had introduced herself. 'My name is Amina and it is the name of the mother of prophet Mohammed, peace be upon Him. In Arabic my name means trustworthy and faithful. I live and work in Sarajevo with the Red Crescent. I don't know how much you know about our wonderful country and how it has been devastated by war. We are a country divided into three parts, Republika Srpska, the Federation of Bosnia and Herzegovina and Brkčo District.'

The theme of the session was Healthy Communication. In the words often attributed to playwright George Bernard Shaw: 'the single biggest problem with communication is the illusion that it has taken place.' Our hope was that in the session people would be able to communicate their feelings and needs with one another and learn new ways of communicating.

Initially, when I spoke to Amina about joining Dodir Nade, I asked her how she felt about us including Christian material.

It is important that Dodir Nade is working for reconciliation and I am committed to that. I am not bothered about whether the material you use is Christian or Muslim or from any other faith.

Healthy communication, the jackal and giraffe

I remembered this conversation as we had our opening meditation, a retelling of the parable of the blind men and the elephant.

Once upon a time there were six blind men. They lived in a town in India. They thought they were very clever. One day an elephant came into the town. The blind men did not know what an elephant looked like but they could smell it and they could hear it. They asked, 'what is this animal like?' Each man touched a different part of the elephant. The first man touched the elephant's body. It felt hard, big and wide. 'An elephant is like a wall,' he said. The second man touched one of the elephant's tusks. It felt smooth and hard and sharp. 'An elephant is like a spear,' he said. The third man touched the elephant's trunk. It felt long and thin and wiggly. 'An elephant is like a snake,' he said. The fourth man touched one of the legs. It felt thick, rough hard and round. 'An elephant is like a tree,' he said. The fifth man touched one of the elephant's ears. It felt thin and it moved. 'An elephant is like a fan,' he said. The sixth man touched the elephant's tail. It felt long and thin and strong. 'An elephant is like a rope,' he said. The men argued. 'It's like a wall!' 'No, it isn't! It's like a spear!' 'No, it isn't! It's like a snake!' They did not agree. The king had been watching and listening to the men. 'You are not very clever. You only touched part of the elephant. You did not feel the whole animal. An elephant is not like a wall, or a spear, or a snake, or a tree, or a fan, or a rope.'

The men left the town still arguing. A little girl heard them and said: 'Each of you is right but you are all wrong, but I know what you are talking about!'

After some minutes silence, Amina opened the conversation:

For me that parable speaks to me about the need to be open to other faiths and to people of no faith if we are to live together in peace. That was how I was brought up in Sarajevo. When the city was under the Ottoman rule, Jew, Christian and Muslim lived next to each other. Mosque, Synagogue, Orthodox and Catholic churches stood side by side. As a youngster there was good and open cooperation between all faiths and we were all open to stories from the Bible. I know your Bible stories and I love celebrating Christmas. I did not know the story of the healing of the paralysed man. As a Muslim I could identify with those in the story who

In spite of our differences

questioned the fact that Jesus forgave the man's sins, as it is God alone who can forgive sins. I too question if Jesus is the Son of God. In the role play, I played the owner of the house and was horrified at the mess caused by the man being let down through the roof. All that paled into insignificance when the man got up and walked out of the door. That had a big effect on me as it gave me hope that I could be healed from my pain. I realise that Jesus is a very special man for Christians. In Islam we do recognise Jesus as a prophet. One of our ground rules is to treat each other with respect. Some of us, including myself, have strong views about our faith but we must not try to impose our beliefs on others.

Aleksandra, a Serb, was 40 years of age, a care worker with older people. She lived in Borovo, a predominantly Serb community near Vukovar.

The parable reminds me of the need to remain humble when we are talking with each other about faith. Sometimes it is easy to fall into the trap of thinking we Orthodox Christians have the monopoly of truth. I agree with Amina. We come from very different backgrounds and both Serbs and Muslims have been through turbulent times.

However, Amina was irritated by that last remark. She thought to herself that it was all very well to mention the word 'turbulent'. 'Just think for a moment what it was like for us in Bosnia.' Besides that, she did not like the word 'humble'. For Amina, there was no humility shown at the number of Muslims killed at Srebrenica. She recalled her feelings of irritation when it came to the listening exercise.

In the course of the listening exercise, Aleksandra was fired up to talk about herself, but little did she know that her 'listeners' (other members of the group), had been briefed by Judith and myself to ignore her completely and have absolutely no eye contact. The point of the exercise was to emphasise the importance of having eye contact in listening.

Aleksandra began speaking:

As a young person, I worked in the famous shoe factory in Borovo. It was established in the Vukovar area in 1933 by Tomaš Bata, a Czech businessman, a pioneer in producing rubber goods. After World War 2 until the 1980s the factory became a very

Healthy communication, the jackal and giraffe

successful manufacturing company which sold and exported footwear and rubber products all over Europe. In its heyday, it produced 20 million pairs of shoes every year as well as manufacturing tyres and related rubber goods. It had a workforce of over 22,000 and over 600 shops. Sadly, the war in 1991 put an end to its business in Vukovar for seven years. Now the output and workforce are greatly reduced. I worked on the shop floor producing shoes. It was like being in a family as hundreds of us all working together for the company. I feel sad to see the company is now so small compared to what it used to be. Nowadays, I work as a paid carer with older people. Yes, it is a complete change of direction for me. But what is interesting is that...

Suddenly she stopped. Tears welled up in her eyes.

Her 'listeners' in the exercise were looking up and down, across the room, behind them and avoiding all eye contact. Aleksandra tried at first to stick to her plan but she became increasingly frustrated at what was happening. At the end of the allotted time, besides the tears she said she felt sick. She had to be helped to get up out of the chair. Amina felt some sympathy for her, especially as she felt that Aleksandra was not a bad listener. Amina could see that the exercise had made Aleksandra question her own abilities as a listener.

Amina likewise had to take part in a similar exercise. Somehow, she had survived relatively unscathed and contained her anger and frustration, at least for now. Amina chose to highlight the siege of Sarajevo in her listening exercise.

Sarajevo was cut off from the 5 April 1992 until the 2 February 1996. It was the longest prolonged blockade in modern history. There was a tunnel that was built into the city and we all worked together through the night and day to get supplies into the city to people trapped in their homes. Everyone was frightened to leave their homes. Leaving one's home exposed one to snipers poised on the hills surrounding the city.

But as she spoke, the listeners shook their heads in denial or disbelief. 'You are lying,' one person said. In the end, Amina had to stop talking as she could not stand any more denials. Amina felt differently to Aleksandra, not as upset yet more and more frustrated at the discussion. Unable to contain her feelings, she

In spite of our differences

suddenly exploded and let rip at the group, shattering the relative calm atmosphere. The whole group was transfixed as Amina spoke.

It is all very well sitting around playing games and doing these exercises, but what we need is accountability and action. I am sick of continually recounting what happened in Bosnia as the pain never goes away.

Judith asked what she meant by 'accountability' and 'action'.

Amina put her head in her hands and in a loud voice cried out:

We need justice. Judith and Clive. Have you not heard about Srebrenica?

Srebrenica is situated in the most easterly region of the Serbian part of Bosnia. Its population is quite small, just under 3,000. The war around Srebrenica began in 1992. By April 1993, the area had been declared 'safe'. Thousands of Muslims were driven there. However, the situation under the control of UN peace keepers, Dutch troops, became worse. Bosnian Serb units led by Ratko Mladić captured Srebrenica on 11 July 1995. At a former battery factory in Potečari, the Bosnian Serb army separated families before the executions. 23,000 Muslim women and young children were separated from the boys and men. They were herded onto buses, a look of terror on their faces. Children were screaming for their dads. Muslim men were ashen with fear. To hear Amina speak was very grim and alarming. Amina recounted how Dutch troops, who were acting as UN Peacekeepers, acceded to Bosnian Serb demands that all refugees be expelled from their base. Hundreds of exhausted Muslim men were caught fleeing over the hills and mountains. Over 72 hours, a systematic massacre followed. In total, 8372 Muslim men were slaughtered.

Judith spoke:

Amina, I hear your cries and the pain, your anger and frustration. How can we help you achieve what you want?

Filip was upset and called out:

Amina is crying out for something we all want, that justice should be done for all the atrocities that have been committed in the conflict over the last few years.

Healthy communication, the jackal and giraffe

Amina, pointing to Aleksandra, was adamant that Serbs needed to take responsibility for what took place at Srebrenica.

Aleksandra shouts out:

Why just me? I had nothing to do with what happened in Bosnia.

But you are still part of that community that committed all those evil acts.

Judith and I reminded the group that we were there not to point the finger at anyone for what may or may not have happened.

We need to remember our ground rules about supporting one another in the quest to live in reconciling ways. Amina has talked about the terrible violence of what happened at Srebrenica and Sarajevo. Aleksandra has mentioned what happened at Vukovar. Terrible atrocities have been committed.

The atmosphere in the room was very tense. Several had tears in their eyes. After a brief break, Judith stepped forward and introduced the second part of the session, namely thinking about Non-Violent Communication.[14] The group would be meeting two animals, the jackal and the giraffe. Judith spoke:

Why is it that on the one hand some people get completely cut off from being compassionate, leading them to behave violently and exploitatively, while on the other hand, what allows some people to stay connected to their compassionate nature, even under the most trying circumstances? The language we use in these circumstances is crucial. Clive and I want to introduce you to a different way of communicating. To help us do this I want to introduce to you two friends.

Each member of the group smiled at the two puppets, introduced by Judith as the jackal and giraffe.

I want you to meet our two friends who will be with us on our journey of reconciliation. The jackal lives close to the ground, is cold hearted, the most calculating of killers, known in African cultures

---

[14] For a full account of Non-Violent Communication, read Rosenberg MB *Nonviolent Communication, A Language of Life* Puddledancer Press 2003

as a trickster. The jackal represents the part of ourselves that thinks, speaks, or acts in ways that disconnect us from our own feelings and needs; and those feelings and needs of others.

The language of non-violence is of the giraffe. It has the largest heart of any land animal and its long neck enables it to see far into the distance, taking the long view. Healthy communication comes from speaking from the heart. It is important to speak from the heart, which is the essence of communication that is termed healthy. This is called giraffe language.

The characteristics of giraffe language are remembering we are all unique, respecting others and ourselves, taking responsibility for our own beliefs, thoughts, feelings and actions. Instead of making demands, it makes requests.

We asked the group to give examples of 'jackal language.'

One Serbian participant said:

I am ashamed to say that in Serbia in 1991, Croats were described as 'inhuman fascists' who used children as shields against bullets. Catholic churches were 'fortresses' and 'arms-caches'.[15] Croats had been subjected to a media campaign by the Serbs in which the language of exclusion had been used.

Snježana shares her own experience of this kind of violent communication from the onset of the war.

Threatening language and even hatred toward Croats was present every single day through the media. It seemed as if the whole nation had to be warned about the evil of Croatia and how Croatian politics can jeopardise the life of the Serbian minority in Croatia. My aunt (my dad's only sister) believed every word that was broadcast and the two of us argued about it a lot.

Judith asked the group about the effects of jackal communication. The words came quickly: *lack of trust, fear, lack of respect, distress, misunderstanding, isolation and separation.* In contrast with that way of communicating, the effects of giraffe communication resulted in *respect, empathy, connection and compassion.* Judith explained:

---

[15] Collin M *This is Serbia calling* p48 Serpent's Tail 2001

Healthy communication, the jackal and giraffe

Just like when learning a language, the important thing is to learn to speak it. We are going to try to learn to speak giraffe language and communicate with one another non-violently. In our following meetings, we shall get to know our puppets. When we speak in the language of the giraffe, the giraffe puppet will nod. When the jackal speaks, so the jackal puppet will nod.

Alexsandra and Amina were confused, asking us for clarity, what it meant to speak giraffe language.

At this point I stood up with my back to the group and looked into a mirror.

Aleksandra turned to Amina and said: 'What on earth is Clive doing now? Has he gone mad? He obviously does not like us and has turned his back on us.'

Others wondered: 'Has Clive had a nervous breakdown? Clive does look tired.'

I said:

Your comments illustrate perfectly how much people read into simple actions. This is the first principle of communicating non-violently: that we concentrate just on what I am hearing or seeing. In fact, all I was doing was looking into a mirror with my back to you all. Use your eyes and ears carefully, which emphasises the importance of listening.

During the break, Aleksandra and Amina decided to walk along the bank of the river Drava. Aleksandra pointed out the other side of the river which, she said led into Baranja and the occupied zone of 1991-5. They walked over the footbridge and saw the children's playgrounds, empty during the bombardment of Osijek. Amina loved the peacefulness of the river, walking in silence along the bank and said:

You have told me that you live near Vukovar. That must be a very difficult place to live and work in because of what happened there in 1991. When we read about the destruction of Vukovar, it sent a shudder down my spine as I knew then that Bosnia would be drawn into the war.

Aleksandra replied:

In spite of our differences

But surely, what happened in Sarajevo and in Bosnia as a whole was far more terrible? I can well understand how frustrated and angry you are with me because of what you have been through.

Amina responded:

All our family in Sarajevo bought our shoes from Borovo. It is interesting to meet someone who actually worked there in the factory. Factories closing because of the war has happened in Bosnia. Unemployment is high in our country. Young people see no future for themselves and so they leave.

The group was keen to help Aleksandra and Amina be at peace with one another. The morning's 'explosion' had disturbed them.

Judith opened up the afternoon session and recapped the conversation from the morning. 'The first part of healthy communication is Observation. The second is Feeling.' Turning to Amina and Aleksandra, I asked how they both felt when they realised that the other two people in the group were not listening to them at all. Aleksandra replied:

At first, I was eager to tell my story. I felt happy and hopeful, but my feelings changed when I realised that the people, whom I thought were listening to me were not. I felt bewildered and very frustrated.

Amina said:

I can identify with what Aleksandra is saying as I had all those feelings and I was brokenhearted and exasperated when the pair of 'so-called' listeners kept on downplaying what I was saying.

Judith explained that when we feel uncomfortable it is a sign of unmet needs. Needs are the third component of non-violent communication. Thinking of all those negative feelings, she asked Aleksandra and Amina what needs were not being met.

Aleksandra said that she had a need for consideration and understanding. Amina thought for a moment and said her needs were for love and respect.

The fourth component of non-violent communication is Request. What requests would they like to make to the group? Both Amina and Aleksandra said that their request was simply that every group member hears, with their whole being, what they were both saying. Amina spoke:

Healthy communication, the jackal and giraffe

My father and brother died in the siege in 1993. They were both shot within months of each other and then my mother died of a broken heart. We Muslims prayed each day that Allah would bring peace and we would be rescued, but nobody came. All around the city of Sarajevo were hills on which snipers were positioned to shoot at individuals who dared to venture out into the open streets. Food and water were scarce. We lived with the fear of being shot dead, but Allah has spared me to tell this story to you. Praise be to Allah.

Aleksandra added:

I find it hard to say how I feel. As a young girl I was never asked how I am feeling and if I did say how I was feeling, I was told by my parents to keep quiet. All this emphasis on feelings is difficult for me. At school we were all told what we must think as opposed to say what we actually felt. We had to toe the party line.

Several people chimed in, *slažemo se* (we agree).

Listening to Amina about her experience in Sarajevo makes me feel guilty but I need to say that when Vukovar was being destroyed, some people shouted at me to leave Croatia and go back to Serbia. I have been living there all my life. Vukovar is my home. I felt upset and angry. Is it any wonder that on the line of health, my score was four, because I am so stressed.

Aleksandra had a lot to think about when she returned to her job as a paid carer. She felt chastened in the listening exercise. Now she is back at work she made a special effort to listen intently to the people in her charge. She also could not forget what Amina had shared about Srebrenica. She went along to the Orthodox Church and lit several candles for Amina and the victims of the Srebrenica massacre.

It was a long way back home for Amina. At first, she was very hard on herself, almost beating herself up for 'exploding' in the session. But then she remembered what Judith and I had said about needs. It was important to recognise our needs and think about how those needs can be met. She thought about the strategies she needed to have in order to meet those needs. At her local Mosque, she gave thanks to Allah for Dodir Nade, and prayed for understanding and patience when meeting Aleksandra.

Chapter 11

Identity

I do not know who I am anymore because of the war. One of the consequences of the war for me has been that I feel I am constantly being asked to be on one side or the other. I cannot sit on the fence. I am being told how I must think and act. But I want to be free to think what I want, not to be told what to think and do what I want to do.

These were the opening remarks by Teodora at 'catch-up time' in the session on identity.

Snježana shared her own experience about the lead up to the war in 1991.

I can understand where you are coming from Teodora. Ethnic hatred grew in Croatia while various incidents by Serbian forces were taking place in parts of Croatia. Suddenly it was very important to identify yourself by your ethnic background. My dad declared himself a Serb and my mom a Croat. I didn't want to identify myself with either of the two. The only important identity for me at the time was to be a child of God. My mother lost her job believing she wouldn't have lost it if my dad wasn't a Serb. My dad lost his position of being General Director of the Post Office (only because of his ethnic background) and had to travel quite far to his new job. Serbian forces had occupied surrounding villages, which were mostly populated with Serbs, and started bombing our town.

Our venue that day was Bizovačke Topilce (Bizovac Spa) just 20km from Osijek. In the background we could hear the noise of children and young people enjoying the 11 pools, some of which were thermal baths. It was a fun place to be and everyone in the group looked forward to relaxing in the pools at some point over the weekend.

Mario, smartly dressed, slightly balding, was emerging as the pastor in the group, and gave a Biblical reflection:

After our discussion last time about language of violence and war, I thought about the verse in the Bible from the book of James: but no one can tame the tongue—a restless evil, full of deadly

Identity

poison. With it we bless the Lord and Father, and with it we curse those who are made in the likeness of God. From the same mouth come blessing and cursing. *(James 3:8-10). We need to watch our language as we work together. Think of how words can lead to powerful inspirational speeches made for the good of the human race, like the 'I have a dream' speech by Martin Luther King. Words can also inspire hate and murder, like the speeches of Adolf Hitler. I agree with Teodora that I am not so sure of who I am anymore. I am confused, because before the hostilities in 1991, Serbs and Croats got on well where we live. Then everything was turned upside down and friends become enemies. The language of war becomes the norm.*

Judith and I explained we would be exploring who we were as individuals and how we can support each other in who we wanted to be. The first task was for everyone to think about the name(s) given to them at birth by their parents. What was the meaning of their name(s)? Did they like their names? Would they like another name? Did they have a nickname?

Teodora was the first to speak. Her name means 'God's gift'.

I do not like my name, because I feel anything but 'God's gift'. I do not feel I have anything to give to anyone, especially now since the war. That is why I placed myself at number 3 on the line of health. My mental health is now so bad after the fall of Vukovar. When the town disintegrated, it was as if I collapsed as well.

Judith and I encouraged her to say more.

I come originally from Pančevo in Serbia, a large town near Belgrade. I met my husband Dušan there. We were childhood sweethearts. Pančevo is an industrial town and Dušan was a chemical engineer working for the petrochemical industry. I trained in Belgrade as a kindergarten worker and got a job in Pančevo. A big opportunity came up for Dušan to work in Vukovar as an engineer and so we moved there. Sadly, the move did not work out for us. Although he enjoyed the job, he found it hard to live in Croatia because of the political tensions in the region in the late '80s. I discovered he was very anti-Croat. I was quite happy to live in Vukovar and made lots of friends. It was a nice town and lovely to live by the Danube. But we grew apart and were divorced just before things really hotted up in Serbia under President

In spite of our differences

Milošević. I had feelings of failure because our marriage broke down. My home town was one of the worst affected in the NATO bombing of 1999. The main chemical complex, which produced petrochemicals and fertilisers was attacked, causing pollution, the effects of which are still around today. I am very mixed up. I am heartbroken that my home town was destroyed and feel angry with the UK for supporting NATO. But I can also see that the fighting in Kosovo had to stop. The NATO bombing brought down Milošević. I am bitterly upset at the fall of Vukovar.

Mario told us his name came from the Latin Marius, widely regarded as a male equivalent to the female Christian name Maria.

I feel humbled to be associated with Mary, the mother of Jesus.

I was surprised to hear that Mario's coming to faith was quite recent. In the line of health, he placed himself in the lower end at 4.

Before I became a committed Christian, I would have thought the state of my health was high at 8 or 9. But I was being unrealistic about myself, so the score of 4 is more accurate.

The groups to which we belong.

The group was now asked to list other groups to which they belonged. This was challenging to Mario because as he did this, he realised there had been a change in his thinking about his identity.

If I had done this exercise ten years ago, I would write that I am a Croat at the beginning of the list. Now, I write that I am a Christian first. Who I am now and what I do is different to, say, ten years ago. I was brought up in Osijek and am the oldest of four children. As a good Croatian family, we were taught to go to Mass every Sunday at the Cathedral of St Peter and St Paul in the city centre of Osijek. I confess that it did not mean much to me, attending mass and going through a liturgy every week in a very parrot fashion way. I was not committed to Christ. We have family in Germany because my uncle was Gastarbeiter (Guestworker) in the '80s in Gelsenkirchen. He had become an attender of an evangelical church and he invited me to come along. My faith in God deepened as I attended the church. I realised that, at that time in my life, my nationality as a Croat was more important than my faith in God.

Identity

Teodora also found the exercise challenging and commented on the different ways people can define themselves. The list seemed never ending: nationality, birth, gender, family, employment, religion, pet owner, interests, sports affiliations, education, accommodation, residence and so on. Teodora said:

What is the most important? Surely it has to be that I am Orthodox? Formerly I would have written the word 'wife,' but now it saddens me to put the word divorcee.

Face mould exercise

The work on oneself deepened with the next part of the session. Having identified the different ways of thinking about ourselves, each person was invited to take a face mould. On one side they were asked to draw symbols or pictures depicting their identity. On the other side, they drew symbols or pictures showing times when their identity was hurt or parts were hidden from view. This activity needed more time and the room fell silent. Then participants talked about their masks in small groups.

Mario drew a big cross in the centre of the mask, with an overarching rainbow symbolising the love and mercy of God. He also drew pictures of his family, a symbol of NK Osijek football team and also of Manchester United. On the reverse side was a picture of an M70 rifle he had used in the war, with the words *Domovini vjerni*, the motto of the Croatian army, 'faithful to the end'. There was a large black line across the rifle. In the corner Mario had drawn a church with a large steeple.

Teodora had drawn a picture of an Orthodox church, a dog, tennis racket, different coloured trees and flowers. On the reverse side was a house with shattered windows and her name in Serbian Cyrillic letters crossed out.

Mario and Teodora were in the same group and they shared with one another. Teodora burst into tears as she talked about the time when her identity was hurt. 'Because I am a Serb my house was stoned and the windows smashed. Priceless items in the house were broken.' In Vukovar, as a reaction against the violent onslaught on the town in 1991, there was a campaign to erase public signage in Serbian Cyrillic letters. Writing her name in Cyrillic letters on the face mask and then crossing it out symbolised for her the desire of some to erase the Serbian Cyrillic script from public view.

Nena explained the background to the public signage issue. The Croatian constitution stated signage could be in several languages to reflect the diverse nationalities of the region. However, there had been protests by Croats in Vukovar about the public use of Serbian Cyrillic letters, leading to violent demonstrations. These resulted in people being asked to come down on one side or the other as to whether they agreed or not to the protests.[16]

Teodora went on to say:

When I was young, all I could think about was getting married and raising a family. To be married was an important part of my identity. The move to Vukovar did not work out as I thought it would. Dušan and I argued a lot and we decided to part. It hurts me to write that I am now a divorcee. The destruction of Vukovar resulted in friends and family being torn apart. So, when I got divorced, I lost a lot of support from Croatian friends as most of them either moved away when the town was under attack or if they stayed in the area, they avoided me because I am Serb. I became isolated and more and more depressed. My two children are now living in Zagreb but one daughter is preparing to move to Germany as she feels Croatia has nothing to offer her.

Mario continued:

I have drawn a picture of a Catholic church. My identity was hurt when I started to attend the evangelical church as this brought me into conflict with my family. They were not happy that I did not want to go to the Catholic church. At that time, I felt that in order to be a good Croatian citizen, I had to attend the Catholic church. But I was more interested in identifying myself more with Christ than with the Catholic church. What hurt me most was the attitude of my parents towards Serbs as a result of what happened in World War 2 between Croats and Serbs. My parents avoided Serbs as much as possible and I am ashamed to say that I went along with that as it was what was expected of me. I felt it was not

---

[16] Since 2015 the town council is under no obligation to have bilingual signs

Identity

the right thing to do to avoid Serbs. The more I delve into my past, the more uncomfortable I feel about myself. That is why I gave myself a low score on the line of health in the first workshop.

Pointing to the rifle, Mario said:

Everything to do with the army service is behind me and I do not like talking about it because it was a painful experience. I don't like to think of myself as a soldier ready to kill. I was pushed into the jaws of war and became a killing machine. I am ashamed to say that at first, I was quite happy to be a soldier. At the back of my mind, I could not help thinking of what happened in World War 2 between Croats and Serbs. I almost began to distrust Serbs. Also, when I saw that Catholic churches were being destroyed in Baranja in 1991 by the Yugoslavian National Army (JNA), my bitterness increased.

Teodora reflected on the fact that she was brought up to believe that Croats were bad, because of what took place in World War 2.

When you are brought up to believe that a person is bad, you start treating that person as bad.

Mario replied:

From my Croatian family background, I have inherited this dislike of Serbs after what I heard about Serbs in the World War 2. I am not surprised that your Dušan was so anti-Croat when you moved to Vukovar. Perhaps I need to draw some prison bars on my mask to indicate being imprisoned by the past?

Stereotypes

Earlier in the session, Nena and Snježana had led a game exploring stereotypes. Each person was asked to wear a label on their back with a particular personality trait or gift written on it, but this was not revealed to the wearer. Group members then mixed and reacted to each other according to what was written on the label. Everyone had to guess what was written on their back. Examples of personality traits and gifts were: lazy, unreliable, bad timekeeper, disorderly, methodical, shouts a lot, talks very quietly, is very fit, cannot cook, good at DIY, bad at DIY, forgetful, anxious, not very intelligent.

The object of the game was to look at the effect of labelling and how this affects our perception of a person. It was fast moving and funny. The point soon came across, that we need to move beyond the label to see the real person and not be seduced by stereotypes. I had the words 'has bad timekeeping' on my back, so group members were constantly reminding me to be punctual or making sure I knew what the time was. I guessed what was written on my back soon enough.

This led very neatly to an exercise on stereotypes. A list of various categories of people was read out and each member of the group was asked to write down the first word that came to mind. The list included politicians and the police, which produced very negative responses. For the words 'English people' several put the word 'cold'. Judith explained that a stereotype contains simplified judgements about a group of people, which leads us to see all members of that group as having certain (usually negative) traits. Judith added that people should not be judged for harbouring stereotypes. It is impossible not to come to some general conclusions about other people based on our limited experience of them. This experience comes through personal contact, the media and the influence and information gained from friends, family and associates. Stereotypes are inevitable, but they are essentially both limited and limiting. The first step in combating their negative influence is awareness.

Who am I and who do I want to be?

Defining the word 'identity' was a challenge. Teodora said she was so mixed up she couldn't think straight. Mario came to the rescue and said: 'Identity is simply who I am and what I do.'

Both Mario and Teodora agreed the workshop on identity was the most important of all. It was in the name of ethnic identity that so many had died and so many people had been displaced in the former Yugoslavia. Through taking part in the exercises, they had discovered more about each other and acknowledged how each felt about the other side. Their honesty had brought them closer to each other. I asked Teodora how she felt about herself now, at the end of the day.

I have been able to say how I feel and to say what I think. I am able to be me. I am uncomfortable to admit I am Serbian, but it is good I can say that.

Identity

There was some disagreement about whether it was a good thing to mention the words 'nationality' and 'religion'. Some said we must not be afraid to declare our nationality whether a person is Serb, Croat, Hungarian or British. Mario said he used to be proud to say he was a Croat, but was not so sure now because of references to World War 2.

I prefer to use the word 'non-aligned' in reference to nationality.

During conversation at the evening meal, Judith and I were asked if we were happy to admit being British? I replied that I often felt very unhappy about it because of atrocities done by the British, particularly in the slave trade.

And I am embarrassed to say I am British because of the decision to leave the European Union.

Subsequent participants repeatedly stressed that the workshop on identity was the most important. The theme was the most important for me too. Thinking about who I am now and the person I was when I became a Methodist minister, my profile now would be very different.

Chapter 12

The Wounded Healer

Dobrodošli svima (welcome everyone). Sajra, with her long dark hair, wearing a sparkling necklace, beamed and welcomed us all to Bosnia.

Friends, the last time we met we were thinking about who we are and who we strive to be. It is also important to know where we live and it is lovely to see you all in our wonderful country. As you can see this hotel stands overlooking the river Una and the river forms the border with Croatia. It joins the river Sava which flows into the Danube in Belgrade. I hope you will find time to visit our lovely town of Bosanska Dubica. We have had turbulent times here in the past but we hope now there will be a lasting peace and I look forward to sharing with you in our work for peace and reconciliation.

Judith and I thanked Sajra for her welcome.

After hearing so much about the country from Amina and Sajra, it is good to actually cross the border and experience Bosnian hospitality. We know that your name means 'happiness, joy and delight' and it is a delight to be here.

Lana had earned the nickname 'ray of light'. This was because her name meant 'light' and she was the youngest member of the group at 37. Bouncing up and down on her chair, she told the group that after the session on identity, she used the face mask exercise with a group of young people in her club in Vukovar.

We had a great time making the masks and then decorating them. The club is mainly Croatian with some Serbs and other nationalities. When we talked about the times when our identity is hurt, one boy shared with us that he is gay and he cannot tell his parents. The one other issue that came up was that we should resist the pressure to say we are of a particular nationality and instead say, 'I am non-aligned.'

Today's session was entitled The Wounded Healer. I reminded everyone of our mission statement: 'motivate, empower and help men and women wounded by war in the process of healing.' The aim of our activities over the weekend was to provide a safe space and time in which to think about our wounds. How could each of us be a healing influence in community? We acknowledged we were all wounded as individuals and as communities.

Exclusion and embrace

The mood was good and positive. Despite the nature of the topic, everyone seemed upbeat. The atmosphere changed quickly as the first exercise got under way. It was called Exclusion and Embrace.

On hearing the title of the exercise, Lana uttered in a loud voice,

That sounds an interesting exercise. I try to be positive and give the young people hope because, without hope, we cannot survive.

On the line of health, Lana had put herself at 8. She was slouching on a sofa but stood to attention as instructions were issued by the leaders. She was wearing jeans and a t-shirt with a huge, happy smiling face on it with the words 'be happy.' She whispered to herself: 'So Clive wants me and everyone else to work around the room in silence greeting one another. This is wonderful, and what a great group. It is difficult to walk around the room and not say anything at all. That's a big ask. But at least we can hug one another.' Everyone sauntered around the room, smiling, high-fiving, hugging one another and making sure everyone was greeted.

'What does he want us to do now?' thought Lana. 'Continue to walk around the room, but ignore one another, avoiding eye-contact? Okay, I think I shall enjoy this time for myself. I shall switch off completely.'

Lana walked in a world of her own, skilfully avoiding other members of the group. As she did so, everyone else also averted their eyes, giving each other a wide berth. Faces were expressionless, heads bowed, arms pinned to the side.

Now what was happening? Lana noticed balls thrown up in the air. She managed to catch one. So did Amina and Filip. 'Apparently, I am able to join those who have a ball, but cannot speak to them. How lucky I am to have a ball and now I have to find others who have one.'

The three who had a ball formed a circle, putting their arms around each other and smiling. Finally, Lana realised it was the last

In spite of our differences

phase of the exercise. It ended as it began. Everyone moving around the room, greeting one another in silence. There was now a noticeable release of tension.

Well, that was a great experience.

Lana spoke in a loud voice. She looked around the group to see a host of blank faces. Some were crying.

After a few minutes I asked the question:

What did you feel and what did you think as you did the first part of the exercise?

Lana replied:

I felt so happy, being together as part of a lovely warm group. We were like children smiling and enjoying ourselves.

But Sajra said:

I felt at peace at first. Embracing one another was healing, but then I sensed that the mood was going to change.

Sajra was right in thinking all was going to change. The instruction to ignore each other made her cry.

I felt excluded, in a dark tunnel and could not get out. I was back in 1992/3 and all the feelings of insecurity came back. When I read about World War 2, about how Jews were treated, something similar happened to us Muslims during the Bosnian war. The exercise reinforced feelings of insecurity and fear. Ignoring others hurt me, especially when some were able to communicate with each other if they managed to catch a ball. Not being able to embrace one another was difficult and being faced with blank expressions was depressing. Although I knew deep down that this was just an exercise, I nevertheless felt excluded.

Viktoria said:

The second stage was awful as it reminds me of how people avoided one another in the street in Vukovar. Our wounds go very deep. Before the war we used to greet everyone normally and chat with each other for hours.

Aleksandra and Teodora nodded in agreement.

slažemo se, *(we agree) that is exactly how we feel after this exercise.*

The Wounded Healer

It is as if I do not exist when a former neighbour sees me coming and then crosses the street because she does not want to talk with me anymore.

Filip and Amina were at first happy to have caught the balls, but then began to feel guilty at being able to smile and be happy. This was at the expense of everyone else, those who had to remain glum and avoid one another. Others were envious towards those who had the balls and could communicate with other members of the group. There was real anger and resentment about the haves and the have-nots in the game.

The group generalised about how in life some have a lot of material possessions and some don't. Some felt many people had profiteered from the war. Others were frustrated about wanting to help others and yet feeling they had to help themselves. Reflecting on the last part of the exercise, several said, in a loud voice:

We were so happy to be greeting each other once more.

We continued with a discussion about what took place in the activity. Several said they did not like doing things in silence. But Lana reacted differently.

I found avoiding each other very helpful as I enjoyed some time and space for myself. We have choices and I chose at that point to withdraw myself completely and was quite happy to switch off from you all.

Lana added she was frustrated people continued to avoid others in the street.

But life is so short, so why can't people say 'let bygones be bygones', and live life as normal?

Sajra said:

Yes, but what happened in Bosnia and in Vukovar has left us all traumatised. Lana you are almost saying you should snap out of it and move on. When you are suffering from PTSD, you can't just move on at the drop of a hat. Have some understanding and empathy as you are young with your whole life before you. Listen to us. Learn from us and let the youngsters you work with know about our situation.

In spite of our differences

For once Lana was quiet and pensive. With tears in her eyes, she ended:

I feel upset by your words Sajra. Leave me alone, I will sort myself out.

The Good Samaritan

After a break, the session moved onto a story about wounds and being wounded; the story of the Good Samaritan. For the purposes of the session, I assumed the Samaritan was himself a wounded person because of the hostility between Jews and Samaritans, which dates back to the 8th century BC.[17]

The group reacted enthusiastically at the suggestion we act out the story. Very quickly the cast and roles were chosen. Elaborate preparations were made for the action and the room was transformed. Jesus entered the room. The group clapped and cheered as he addressed the lawyer and the crowd. All looked expectantly at the lawyer.

'Teacher, what must I do to inherit eternal life?'

Jesus replied, 'What is written in the law? What do you read there?'

The lawyer recites the law, then Jesus says: 'You have given the right answer: do this, and you will live.'

Then came that important question for us all,

'And who is my neighbour?'

The action then unfurled. The victim walked across the large room, carefully, down the winding road from Jerusalem to Jericho, at the side of which were boulders and bushes. Suddenly, there was pandemonium. Everyone jumped as masked robbers appeared. With some ferocity they forced the hapless traveller to the ground, beating him mercilessly. There was a gasp of horror as the man was left on the ground, fighting for his life. A deathly silence fell. A few minutes later, which seemed like hours, a priest came by looking very pious, holding a book of prayers. He took one look at the

---

[17] The Samaritans did not recognise Jerusalem as the centre of worship. In wars with the Jews, they sided with the Syrians and were against the restoration of Jerusalem. We also explain that a Levite is a descendant of the tribe of Levi and they assisted priests in the temple or tabernacle.

victim on the road, pointed his nose in the air and speedily moved on. Then Lana, who played the Levite, walked by looking even more pious holding a service book, reciting prayers in a monotone. Taking one look, she too walked on quickly. As the priest and Levite passed by, the victim on the ground lifted up his arm as if pleading for succour, gasping for water. This was too much for one member of the group, who moved toward the victim. Lana whispered: 'For God's sake, get back. It is only a role play it is not real life.'

After a long silence, Sajra the Samaritan appeared. She stopped, sighing deeply. Bending over the injured man, she washed his face, binding his wounds. The waiting donkey sidled up to him and together they walk to the inn. At first, the innkeeper was reluctant to take the injured man, because of his bloodied wounds. Moreover, the victim's saviour is a Samaritan. 'I have my reputation to think of. What will people make of me having dealings with a Samaritan?' Eventually, the innkeeper agreed to take him, but only when he saw the huge amount of money he would receive. He was even happier at the thought of more money, should there not be enough. The donkey was pleased to have carried the injured man to safety. 'It will be good practice for me as I have another important journey. Soon, I am to carry Jesus into Jerusalem'.

Jesus turned to his hearers and asked: 'Which of these three was a neighbour to the man who was robbed?'

'The one who showed him mercy.'

At this the hearers gasped in horror and fell to the ground in shock, muttering among themselves. 'A Samaritan showing mercy? No way, how can it be?'

Jesus said, 'Go and do likewise.'

For a moment there was silence, then everyone stood and clapped. The victim struggled to his feet and was helped into a chair. We all took a break.

The room was buzzing. Judith and I were impressed by the enthusiasm of the group, how they'd put heart and soul into acting out the parable. I told them the Royal Shakespeare Company in Stratford-upon-Avon was always looking for new actors.

After asking the characters to stay in their roles, Lana was the first to speak.

In spite of our differences

I really enjoyed that play as I love acting. I have to admit that I had to try really hard not to laugh as I played my character. I held my head up high as I passed the victim, took one look and hurried on as I had very important tasks to perform that day. I could not help turning up my nose at the victim, for after all as a priest I must not touch anyone who is unclean. In any case, I was so busy having to get to a meeting and I was running late. The man was rather stupid to be walking down that road, as it was known to be unsafe for travellers.

Sajra's face reddened and her body tensed up at Lana's apparent flippancy. She, of course, had played the Samaritan. In contrast to Lana, the play had affected her deeply. Sajra could not get over the shock that people expressed when she, the Samaritan, was identified as the one who had helped the injured man on the road.

I think of the game we played in the session on identity, when we all had labels on our backs. We had to treat one another according to the labels. I think the shock on people's faces comes from the fact that Samaritans were regarded as the lowest of the low by Jews. When the Samaritan is identified as the one who showed mercy, people did not believe that this can be so. What upsets me is it reminds me of how I was treated in the war as a Muslim. There was so much prejudice against Muslims by Serbs and Croats that few people expected anything good to come from a Muslim. Yet Islam is a religion of peace, so why should I not be the one who shows mercy?

Lana felt increasingly uncomfortable as the mood in the group darkened.

I feel out of my comfort zone here. I am ashamed to say that I did not know all this was going on with Muslims being targeted in the way you said. My pain is so much less than yours, Sajra. However, I do care. I too have had my share of hurt. I was very young when the war broke out and my mother and father took me to stay with family on the coast. I did not understand what was going on. The worst thing was to see my parents crying uncontrollably. When it was safe to do so, we all returned to our village, but there were a lot of destroyed properties and many people had left. My parents were upset but I found it hard to express my feelings, because I did not want to upset them anymore. I felt I had to be in charge of the housekeeping as they were not coping at all.

Lana described her own wounds:

In the war, we had to leave our house suddenly. We could only take essential things with us, so I just took some toys and books. When we arrived at the coast, we were crammed in to our relative's house. Things were very tense because there were so many people in a small space. I went outside to play with other children but they were not very friendly and told me to go back to Osijek. It was then I realised how much I missed my own home and friends, and I began to get upset. People can be so horrible and uncaring.

For me it is important to hear about the experience of the war from those who fought and those who have been wounded both physically and psychologically. It is important to listen to those who are older than me. I have to confess that I am impatient and people do not move on as fast as I would like. Sajra's experiences are reminding me how deep the wounds of war are and there are no quick fixes. My big concern is to work with young people on conflict prevention so that fighting does not break out again. This region is a great area in which to live and I want to encourage young people to stay here rather than go abroad.

Lana addressed Sajra.

Talking in your role as a Samaritan, how is it that you are able to help the victim even though you are wounded yourself?

Sajra said quietly:

I wonder myself what motivated the Samaritan to be so kind. Personally, I can see that when a person is wounded, that person is faced with lots of choices in the way to react. I could have been filled with revenge and killed him. I could have laughed and mocked him. It was the sight of blood that drew me to him and I just knew I had to help him.

Lana interrupted Sajra to say she felt badly now for not having shown compassion for the victim. I remarked that now the lines between actor and person are blurred. The story had affected Sajra and Lana deeply. Lana's and Sajra's wounds were laid bare. Sajra confided that during the role play she'd remembered her Good Samaritan in the camp.

I was spat upon and sexually abused continually. One of the guards told me I was going to be killed and I cried and cried. I begged that someone would help me. There was one man who did. He was one of the guards. He told the others that I was ill and should go to hospital. In fact, I recognised him as he was a friend of my husband from a nearby village. By the mercy of Allah, I was singled out and went to hospital and I was spared. That man was my Good Samaritan.

Lana and Sajra embraced.

Mario was thankful to God there were good people ready to say no to violence. This prompted Judith to ask: 'Who are the wounded healers for each of us, people who have been wounded yet are able to be a channel of healing for us and others?'

Snježana's experience

Snježana shared her story of being wounded after bearing the scars of not being encouraged to go to Church from her early years. Her parents were atheists and members of the League of Communists of Yugoslavia.

We never went to church or spoke about God, since God didn't exist in our home.

When she came to faith, things became even more difficult.

My mother's reaction to my expression of love for God was: 'I feel like you just slapped me!'

Her mother said believing in God was only for poor and illiterate people, not for them.

My dad gave me the most serious lecture about how he could lose his position within the Party, once people found out his daughter was a believer. And I knew that was true since I remember this one time the Catholic wedding ceremony was performed for our friends. We all went in the church and my dad stayed outside and smoked his cigarette. He didn't like the fact his wife dared to go in. I was strictly forbidden to attend church or to mingle with the church members. I had to hide my first and only The book of Christ *under my bed covered with the carpet. If I decided to sneak out to the church service in spite of the ban, I had to make up different reasons for being away. Former communist party members who had become Christians supported me, even though they too were mocked by people outside the Church.*

Somebody mentioned Nelson Mandela, who in his book *Long Walk to Freedom* writes about the wounds he received as a youngster growing up in the apartheid system in South Africa. He suffered more wounds in prison. Yet despite being so wounded he showed great magnanimity to his jailers, and to those who mistreated him in prison.

To finish the discussion, the question was asked: Who are the despised people in our communities today? Some suggested the Roma population, because few people had a good word to say about them. This does not surprise me, because of the widespread discrimination in the region against Roma in housing and employment.

The prayer for healing was more important than ever today as the activities had been quite exhausting and emotionally demanding. I began with a short reflection on how, when we are seeking to live in reconciling ways, we often look for models and techniques. Jesus lived in a reconciling way in the manner in which he came alongside people and was present with them. Jesus's ministry had roots in grace, expressed primarily through the quality of presence: the way he chose to be present, in relationships and in the company of others, even those who wished him harm. A weight of heaviness descended upon me as I said the prayer for healing for each person.

However, after the prayer for healing, there was a lightness, as if a breath of wind had blown through the room. We spent our last moments together being present with each other, by giving one another an imaginary present, miming to the person sitting next to us. Some of the presents included a big bunch of flowers, a lovely meal in a restaurant, new clothes, happiness, and for me, as a bus enthusiast, a big red London bus. Judith was given some vegetable seeds for her garden. Then, we made our way to the restaurant.

Chapter 13

Forgiveness

This weekend we were exploring forgiveness. Once again, we had crossed a border, this time into Serbia, meeting in the city centre of Novi Sad. Novi Sad is a beautiful city, the second largest city in Serbia with a population of 300,000, on the north shore of the Danube. This part of Serbia is called Vojvodina, meaning Duchy or Dukedom. The area north of the Danube belonged to the Austrian Empire. After the battle of Mohács in 1526, now in present day Hungary, the area came under the control of the Ottomans until the late 17th century when it became part of the Habsburgs. Overlooking the river Danube in Novi Sad is the Petrovaradin Fortress, which was extensively enlarged and fortified after the defeat of the Ottomans in 1692. After this defeat, many different nationalities moved to the area such as Hungarians, Croats, Romanians, Slovaks, Germans, Roma and Ruthenians from the Ukraine. This makes the region the most multi-ethnic and, from the point of view of the Christian faith, it is the most ecumenical part of Serbia. It even has a small but significant Methodist church.

We were enjoying the hospitality of the Novi Sad Methodist Church. It is near the city centre in a gated courtyard with a chapel and hall with flats for the minister and others above. We were welcomed warmly by the minister, Novica Brankov, with drinks and snacks. For most of the group it was their first contact with the Methodist Church and they were intrigued to know Novica's faith journey.

I have not always been a Methodist – I was brought up in a Serbian Orthodox family in which Orthodox customs and traditions were respected. I attended a Methodist youth camp. It was there that I heard the Word of God for the first time and free prayer. It was the first time that I felt real Christian love, which I could not find in the Orthodox Church. As far as my family were concerned, I was a heretic and sectarian. Soon after, I was playing football a lot and became semi-professional. It was something my father did not understand, because I earned a lot from the football. He told me I was being influenced by a sect. It was not easy for me

Forgiveness

as a Protestant and Methodist member to live in an Orthodox family. I was often mocked. I had to leave my friends with whom I played football. This situation lasted about three years. After three years my mother joined the Methodist Church, also my brother, my father after eight years. Now, a couple of cousins and my brother's family are members of the Methodist Church.

Despite the warm welcome, Judith and I were apprehensive about leading a workshop in Novi Sad. In 1999, there were NATO attacks on the city to put pressure on President Milošević to end fighting in Kosovo. Three bridges, Zezeljev, Freedom and the bridge that connected Novi Sad with Petrovaradin Fortress, were hit. This last bridge, the Varadinski Bridge, connected the Serbian Orthodox world on the one side with the Catholic world on the other. Children from the Serbian side were used to crossing the bridge to get to school. An oil refinery was also targeted, with a disastrous result for the environment, as the explosions released dangerous chemicals into the atmosphere. The water and electricity supplies were hit as well. All this had dire consequences for the physical health of the residents. To this day, the NATO bombing of Novi Sad is controversial. When it took place, the city was ruled by the Democratic opposition, which was firmly opposed to the Belgrade regime. The fighting at the time was in Kosovo, situated in the southern end of the country. Citizens of Novi Sad could not understand why their city was targeted. In 2025, there is still controversy over the death toll. No exact figures have been published and there is no list of civilian names. This lack of information feeds politicians manipulating the situation.

We had our catch-up time. Milena and Ivana had become friends through playing the robbers in the Good Samaritan role play. They had not liked to say so at the time, but they realised how much it served their purpose to attack the man journeying along the road. Milena said:

I am ashamed to say that as the man walked across the room in the play, I felt real aggression. I put that down to the angry feelings I have in my life because of the war. I was letting my own feelings out and it was good.

In the first session, Milena had introduced herself as;

In spite of our differences

Sadly Serbian, 54 years old. I live in Borovo and I work in Vukovar as a science teacher in a secondary school. I have two teenagers, a boy and a girl, who are living away in Germany with relatives. I did not want them to stay in Croatia and they are better off in Germany, but I miss them terribly. On the line of health, I gave myself a score of 3 because of my low self-esteem.

Likewise, Ivana said she experienced a certain amount of satisfaction attacking the man but then felt very guilty. In the first session Ivana told us:

I am 43 years, Croat, work as a primary school teacher in Osijek. I am happy to be here, learn new things and meet new people. I went to the Catholic church until the war started, but now I do not believe there is a God.

Both Milena and Ivana asked for forgiveness from the 'victim' who had been played by Aleksandra. 'I am completely shocked,' she said, 'that you ask now for forgiveness. Does this mean you have been carrying this guilt all this time?' Smiling, Aleksandra added: 'Of course, I forgive you.' Milena and Ivana nodded and looked at each other sheepishly.

Responses to hurt

Still smarting from a seeming rebuke by Aleksandra, they realised that the session was moving on to the first exercise; being asked to say how they reacted when they are hurt. 'How do you feel and what do you do when somebody hurts you?' Judith asked.

The responses were varied. Judith and I grouped the reactions into four sections. Subsequently four groups were formed; revenge, avoidance, forgiveness and authentic reconciliation. Each group was asked to form a statue representing each of the sections. The tasks were to say what each heading felt like, looked like and sounded like. The second part of the exercise was to form a statue depicting the name of the group.

Revenge was represented by clenched fists and angry looks. Feelings were described as 'running high, angry and tense.' The language was violent, recriminatory and hostile. Avoidance was shown by the group facing away from one another with ears and eyes covered. The body language was limp, with glum looks. The language was flat, negative and dismissive. Forgiveness was

Forgiveness

shown by open arms, the language conciliatory with feelings of relief. Authentic reconciliation was depicted as a group embrace, all facing outwards because the future was wide open. The words used were 'let us work together on building a new relationship.' Feelings expressed were positive.

The groups were chosen at random and Milena found herself in the Forgiveness group and Ivana in Reconciliation. The irony was that neither of them wanted to be in either group.

Ivana said:

I ought to be thinking about reconciliation, but if I am honest, I am drawn to the revenge group. I am so angry and sometimes I wonder why I have come on these workshops. I am drawn to the clenched fists rather than the group facing outwards.

Milena admitted:

I feel the same. I feel obliged to stand in the forgiveness section but do not feel very forgiving.

Other members of the group expressed similar feelings, saying they did not automatically feel they wanted to forgive.

Being realistic, when we are hurt and traumatised, we experience so many different kinds of feelings and emotions and do not readily fall into one particular group of reactions.

Judith waved the jackal puppet in the air at the mention of the words 'obliged' and 'ought'.

'Stick with what you are feeling and what you are needing at this point.'

At this point, I asked the question: what is forgiveness? In small groups the following words were noted:

Communication, consideration, relief, ok, I am sorry, uncomfortable, I did not think like that, empathy, I did not do it on purpose, forgetting, tolerance, joy, a new beginning, helping ourselves, love, understanding, new day, new opportunity, move on.

To help our understanding, I offered the group a definition of the word. 'Forgiveness is the ending (renunciation or cessation) of resentment, anger as a result of a (perceived) offense, disagreement or mistake or ceasing to demand punishment or restitution.'

Milena said:

In spite of our differences

If that is what is meant by forgiveness, then clearly, I am not ready to forgive. I am struggling with this theme, Clive.

To close the evening, each person was asked to say in one word how they were feeling. The dominant word was 'apprehensive'. I was not surprised, because forgiveness is the most difficult of themes on the workshops. The aim is simply to explore forgiveness – as facilitators we are not telling participants they must forgive. To choose to forgive another person is up to an individual and nobody can be forced to forgive.

The next morning, instead of opening the session with a meditation, I invited the group to lead our thoughts on forgiveness with a brief acting out of the parable of the Unforgiving Servant in Matthew 18:21-35. Milena, nicknamed 'the teacher', gathered the group together with just 20 minutes to come up with the role play.

Peter asked Jesus: 'If a member of the church sins against me, how often should I forgive? As many as seven times?'

Jesus said to him: 'Not seven times, but I tell you, 77 times.'

Peter carried a card with a number seven written on it. Jesus carried a card with the number 449.

The king (Milena) pretended to do some adding up and sent an official (Viktoria) to the servant (Lana). The servant listened and threw his hands up in horror when he was ordered the pay a debt of 10,000 talents. His wife (Sajra) and child (Filip) sobbed their hearts out. The servant went down on his knees, begging his master for patience, promising to pay everything he owed. Waving his hands up and down he was totally distraught. The king however, smiled and lifted up his hands, blessing the servant as he was released. The servant leapt for joy, embracing his wife and child.

But the same servant noticed another servant (Aleksandra), who owed him 100 denarii. Seizing him by the throat, he said: 'Pay what you owe.' This other servant implored him on his knees, begging for time to pay.

The king's other servants heard what had happened and told the king, who was very angry. The king ordered the servant to be brought to him immediately. *You wicked slave! I forgave you all that debt because you pleaded with me. Should you not have had mercy on your fellow-slave, as I had mercy on you?* In anger, he delivered him to the jailers (Teodora and Ivana).

Forgiveness

For Milena, this parable was too much and she regretted attending the session.

I can so identify with Peter wanting to keep a score of how many times a person should forgive. It seems a very natural thing to want to keep a score and after so many times to say 'enough is enough'. I have given my husband so many opportunities to change. But as for me, I cannot forgive my husband. For me, it all started some time ago when we drifted apart. I discovered that my husband Mihail was having an affair. I was busy at school and with our children, and he was busy in his job as a telephone engineer, often working away with his job. I discovered that instead of doing his work, he was with another woman. I found it hard to forgive him then, but worse was to come.

Ivana responded to Milena.

The marriage relationship depends on mutual trust. Forgiveness must be the last thing on your mind?

Milena replied:

It takes two to make a marriage and if I am honest, I feel guilty about not recognising his needs. It is hard to forgive myself.

Ivana said:

That's ironic, as my problem is that I too can't forgive myself, no matter how hard I try.'

Pat and Jo

Having looked at a biblical story and thought about the nature of forgiveness, it was time to look at real-life example of forgiveness. Judith and I played the parts of Jo Berry and Pat Magee.

'A man of exceptional cruelty and inhumanity,' were the words used by the judge to describe IRA member Pat Magee at his trial in September 1986, for his part in planting a bomb at the Grand Hotel, Brighton in 1984. The bomb attack killed five and injured 54 people. One of the victims killed was the MP, Sir Anthony Berry, whose daughter is Jo.

Jo and Pat's story was part of a growing collection of stories from the resources of the Forgiveness Project.[18]

---

[18] theforgivenessproject.com

In spite of our differences

I have heard Jo and Pat speak publicly about their journeys of forgiveness and reconciliation and talked with them as well. The role play, between Judith and me, was based on what Pat and Jo have written for the Forgiveness Project. Jo writes and Judith says:

I felt as if a part of me died in that bomb. I was totally out of my depth, but somehow, I held on to a small hope that something positive would come out of the trauma. I wanted to meet Pat to put a face to the enemy, and see him as a real human being. At our first meeting I was terrified, but I wanted to acknowledge the courage it had taken him to meet me.

Milena reacted strongly:

I cannot understand the reasons why Jo wanted to meet Pat. Her father died as a result of the bomb in the hotel. Any normal person would have wanted to lock Pat away and throw away the keys to his cell. Pat Magee has committed far worse crimes than my husband and yet here is Jo wanting to meet with him.

Ivana said:

I would be scared if a person I had wronged wanted to meet with me and yet, this is what happened. Jo wrote to Pat and that letter had a powerful effect on him. They decided to meet. It seems to me unbelievable that Jo and Pat sat together for three hours during which time Pat shared why he joined the IRA.

Milena said:

For Jo, the important thing for her was to understand Pat's motivation. That is a challenge for me because of my own situation with my husband. You see, not only has my husband had an affair with another woman, but he is also serving a prison sentence for war crimes. Because of his job, he did not have to fight for the Yugoslav National Army (JNA). It was a terrible time as our children went away to relatives in Germany. When the fighting stopped, the police came to our house and took him away. Mihail said that he had to go to the police station to help with some enquiries, but he did not return. Weeks later, I discovered he had been arrested for suspected war crimes. He was tried and sent to prison. I have had hardly any contact with him and I have now filed for divorce. I just cannot forgive him, first because of his infidelity and second because of his war activities. I am ashamed of

Forgiveness

him. *What is even harder, is the fact that people in my neighbourhood will not speak to me. Several people have shouted outside my house that I should leave Croatia and go back to Serbia. It is hard on my children to stay here, so I arranged for them to go to Germany. Why did Mihail get involved with a terror group? We always got on so well with our Croatian neighbours.*

Ivana:

What resonates with me is when Judith said the question is always about whether I can let go of my need to blame and open my heart enough to hear Pat's story and understand his motivations. The truth is, sometimes I can, and sometimes I can't. For me forgiveness is a journey, a choice, which means it's not all sorted and put away in a box. Now, is my confession time.

The group was all ears.

I have not planted a bomb, but I took part in anti-Serbian activities in Osijek. There was this Serbian family and we tried to get the family of five out of their house. I did not kill anyone but was just very unkind to them. With others we pelted stones at their house and shouted at them to leave Croatia. I feel as if I should be asking that family for forgiveness as I was really violent towards them. In the story of Pat and Jo it was noted that Pat did not ask for Jo's forgiveness. My difficulty is that I cannot forgive myself. I let myself down by getting involved in those anti-Serb activities. I regret the things I did to that family.

As Milena and Ivana were talking, the rest of the group was restless, quite divided in their attitude towards Pat and Jo, directed at Judith and me. Some were angry with Jo for even wanting to meet with Pat. Others insisted Pat ask forgiveness from Jo. As Judith and I came to the close of the story, two of the women, Aleksandra and Milena, are angry with Judith.

We can't understand how you can even contemplate trying to understand Pat.

Judith and I felt very uncomfortable at being in the firing line. I spoke up:

I wish you could all meet Jo and Pat. We have heard them speak a few times and have met with them. When they appear together at a public meeting, I have always been inspired because of the honesty and sincerity of their dialogue. The feelings they have about what happened are very raw and I sense their struggle.

Ivana said:

What I find so inspiring about Jo, is the fact that she has an almost daily battle in which she has to decide whether she chooses the road of forgiveness. I identify with Jo because I find it so hard to even begin to forgive.

Milena said:

Their story seems to me a very hopeful story of reconciliation because Jo's letter requesting a meeting with her made a big impression on Pat. He felt both a political and moral obligation to contribute to the Peace Process, deciding to accede to Jo's request. This journey of reconciliation for them both began. If that can happen for Jo and Pat then it can possibly happen for others who have been caught up in terrorism.

Pat received eight life sentences but was released from prison in 1999, having served 14 years, under the terms of the Good Friday Agreement.

It's rare to meet someone as gracious and open as Jo. She's come a long way in her journey to understanding; in fact, she's come more than half way to meet me. That's a very humbling experience. (The F Word: Stories of Forgiveness.)

Forgiveness ritual

The last part of the session came from Archbishop Desmond Tutu of South Africa, his book *The Book of Forgiving*. Tutu writes that he feared a bloodbath of revenge and retaliation after Nelson Mandela was released from prison in 1990. However, the path of forgiveness was chosen and a Truth and Reconciliation Commission was set up. For Tutu, the concept of Ubuntu, (humanity) is key: our humanity is bound up in one another.

To walk the path of forgiveness is to recognise that your crimes harm you as they harm me. To walk the path of forgiveness is to recognise that my dignity is bound up in your dignity, and every wrongdoing hurts us all.[19]

---

[19] Tutu D&M *The Book of Forgiving* p8 William Collins 2014

Forgiveness

For Tutu, a sign of being healthy is to choose the path of forgiveness, which sets us free from the past, from those who hurt us, offering new beginnings. This creates a ripple effect of healing to family and the wider community. Tutu proposed a Stone Ritual, which we used to meet the needs of people who were looking for some practical guidance in wanting to forgive. We had thought about the nature of forgiveness and heard a case history. Now was the chance for individuals to reflect on forgiveness in their own way.

Participants found a stone they could carry round and interact with. The first activity was to tell the story of what happened to them, in as much detail as possible. Milena related her story to a stone she found on the shore of the Danube.

I remember finding out about my husband being with another woman. We were not relating very well but I still loved him. I found out through a friend who had spotted them in another village close by.

Milena then named the hurt by taking the stone in her dominant hand and saying out loud

I am betrayed, my body aches with pain.

She clenched the stone and her hand opened. As the stone is released, her hurt was released.

The third part of this ritual was to grant forgiveness. Tutu invited everyone to dip their stone in water three times, leaving a long time between each dip into the water. Each time a person dipped the stone in water, the words 'I forgive you' were uttered. But Milena was unable to grant forgiveness and said instead:

I want to try to understand the reasons why you joined the rebels.

Tutu also suggests a sandy place where the person writes a hurt in the sand. Some people elected to do this and went out to the shoreline where there was some sand. They were asked to think of three attributes they valued in the person they wanted to forgive, and write them on a stone. What is written in the sand will disappear, but what is written on stone will remain.

The last part of the ritual concerned Renewing or Releasing the relationship.

In spite of our differences

Ivana said:

I now have to decide whether the stone is to be transformed into a thing of beauty or to be returned to the earth. But I decide to turn the stone into a thing of beauty by decorating it. I am going to take the stone and sit down in the room and start to decorate the stone.

Other participants were keen to show their decorated stone and speak about a renewal in the relationship with the person who caused the hurt.

Sunday morning on this workshop was different. Novica had invited me to preach at the morning service. Our group swelled the small congregation. Novica asked me to talk about Dodir Nade. Referring to the healing of the paralysed man, I emphasised the man's deepest need of forgiveness. On the spur of the moment, I asked if anyone from the group would like to speak. To my delight and surprise Ivana took up the challenge. Her words were like music to my ears. The Absolution, your sins are forgiven, meant a lot to her, she said, adding how surprised this reaction had made her, because she was an agnostic.

Those words bring peace to my soul. I am part of the multi-national group exploring healing and reconciliation. I am a Croat. I confess that I have not always been kind to Serbs, so I ask your forgiveness. Although we come from different sides and backgrounds, we are committed to working together. Dodir Nade has reaffirmed my belief in God.

After the service we met together to talk with the congregation over drinks. Many people thanked Ivana for her words. There was laughter and the inevitable group photo. It was a lovely end to an exhausting weekend.

Chapter 14

Living in a reconciling way

We were at the Red Cross Centre in Orahovica, a delightful small town, one hour from Osijek by car. It was a well-equipped centre, complete with swimming pool, lovely grounds and perfectly-manicured lawns. Our two workers, Nena and Snježana, who grew up in the town, recalled the fighting in the area in 1991.

Serbian forces had occupied surrounding villages, which were mostly populated with Serbs, and started bombing our town. The Croatian National Guard were using the Red Cross resort as their seat which was only 30 metres away from our house. Our house was somehow in the middle of the war lines. We couldn't go to school or work and full blackout was demanded by the local authority. We didn't use any electrical lights – only candles and flashlights. We covered the windows with thick blankets and didn't go anywhere at night. Shelling toward and away from the direction of our house was going on day and night.

Even after such a vivid description, it was hard to imagine fighting had taken place there. Attached to our workshop room was a balcony with stunning views of the town and surrounding countryside, hills in the distance, trees in full bloom, radiant flowers, lush green grass. Everything looked so peaceful.

Our first task, as always, was to ask the group if there were any issues outstanding from the previous session on Forgiveness.

Ivana was first to speak. In fact, she was burning to do so.

I just wanted to say how impressed I was with the pastor at the Methodist Church in Novi Sad. I was moved by his story of how he was brought up in the Orthodox Church and how he came to be in the Methodist Church. It upset me when he talked about the difficulties he had with his family when he joined the Methodist Church. I was happy when he told us how members of his family were now also in the Methodist Church. It was a nice story of forgiveness and reconciliation.

Milena, however, was tearful and in sombre mood.

In spite of our differences

The good news is that I value the story about Jo and Pat. The bad news is that my struggle with wanting to forgive, yet not being able to forgive my husband, is tortuous. I just cannot forgive him. He has brought dishonour on to the name of our family.

We had now come to the final session with its theme of living in a reconciling way. I prefer to use the verb, reconciling, as opposed to the noun reconciliation to emphasise the need to actively work at relationships. This also acknowledges that reconciliation is a journey, which will have setbacks as well as leaps forward.

Filip sighed.

I am sad this is our last meeting together.

Everyone concurred. After finding our rooms, we walked through the grounds to the main block, where we had our evening meal together. After some games and a quick run through the timetable, there was time for a swim, for those who wished. A children's group was also meeting at the main block and we heard them laughing and singing folk songs.

The laughter of the children also greeted us over breakfast. Lana reminded us all of the importance of working with children and young people to encourage them to find non-violent ways of resolving conflict. Deep in discussion, we suddenly realised we were due to start the session.

The meeting

Judith and I explained we were now going to look at a particular way of understanding living in a reconciling way, from the writer John Paul Lederach. He was a grass-roots peace worker, part of a conciliation team in Nicaragua in the 1980s. Lederach was seeking to bring the Sandinistas leaders of the Nicaraguan government together with the resistance, the Miskito leaders. The aim was to end a war that had been waging for almost eight years. It was a fearful time for Lederach and his family. This made him question his own involvement in peace making. He writes from a faith perspective as he is a member of the Mennonite Church, in the Anabaptist tradition. Members are committed to the values of non-violence, resistance and pacifism. He brings freshness and originality to the interpretation of scripture. He is an academic, a professor of international peacebuilding, at home in university circles, but he is able to communicate easily and clearly in an accessible way.

In his book *Reconcile*, Lederach presents an understanding of reconciliation which is based on Psalm 85:10 *Truth and Mercy have met together. Justice and Peace have kissed.*

At the beginning of each day of Lederach's negotiation in Nicaragua, there was a prayer and a reading from the Bible. One morning, Psalm 85 was read and verse 10 stood out.

The concepts kept dancing through my mind as I watched the peace process unfold in fits and starts. For the first time, I noticed that the psalmist seems to treat the concepts as if they are alive. I could hear their voices in the war in Nicaragua. In fact, I could hear their voices in any conflict. Truth, Mercy, Justice and Peace were no longer just ideas, they became people, and they could talk.[20]

Truth, Mercy, Justice and Peace were not seen as adversaries and contradictory; but rather that each saw the place and need for the other.

The first task of the group was for the four voices – Truth, Mercy, Justice and Peace – to have a conversation. The group split into four, each part representing a voice. Then each group considered the meaning of each word. The theme was: How do we live in a reconciling way? The group drew on Lederach's words, and on their own. Some postcards depicting different scenes were also to hand, which members of the group could use to illustrate what was said. Each group chose a symbol.

For Filip, Milena and Lana, Truth was *telling it as it is, reality, honesty, finding out, clarity, often painful, confession, liberating.*

For Teodora, Mario and Amina, Mercy was *forgiveness, new start, acceptance, compassion, letting go, healing.*

For Sajra and Ivana, Justice was *right relationships, making things right, accountability, restitution, repentance.*

Lastly Viktoria and Aleksandra thought Peace was *harmony, well-being, security, good relations.*

---

[20] John Paul Lederach *Reconcile* p83-92 Herald Press 1999

In spite of our differences

There were five empty chairs, one for each of the characters, and one for the narrator, whom the group decided should be Milena. She introduced the conversation.

We have all experienced conflict over the last few years and we have heard the voices of Truth, Mercy, Justice and Peace. Psalm 85:10 tells us: Truth and Mercy have met together. Justice and Peace have kissed. *What does that mean for us here today as we try to live in a reconciling way?*

A representative of each group entered and sat on a stool. They took a bow as the rest of the group clapped. Different members of each group came and went or sat on chairs.

Narrator *Welcome* (acknowledging each and shaking hands).

Truth (Filip was carrying a mirror) *A mirror shows one exactly the way that something is. I am Truth. In times of conflict, I want to bring forward what really happened, putting it out in the open. Dodir Nade has enabled me to face the truth about myself. I realised when I played that paralysed man, how cut off I was from my feelings. It was not a man's job to work on myself. Speaking the truth has meant that we must be honest with ourselves and each other. But the problem is that when it comes to finding out the truth about what happened at places like Ovčara or Srebrenica, people are not so eager to tell the truth. In these places, for example, Ovčara, truth is hidden. People cover up the facts, and the media has different versions of the facts, which are based on politics.*

Narrator (comes forward) *How is that in a conflict, each side will claim that truth is on their side? Truth is elusive and difficult to find.*

Truth (Lana) *I am in agreement with the statement 'truth does appear elusive' and as a young person, I am confused about what I was taught in school about our recent history. So how do I find the truth?*

(Filip) *Surely it is a case of searching for the truth and not giving up. You need to be persistent. For me these sessions have been about being open to the truth about ourselves and what happened in the war.*

Narrator *Of these three friends, whom do you fear the most?*

Truth *We fear Mercy.*

Living in a reconciling way

Narrator (turning toward Truth) *Why?*

Truth *Mercy sometimes obscures the Truth and is too quick to forgive.*

Narrator *Mercy, what do you have to say?*

Mercy (Mario, wearing a symbol of joined hands around his neck). *Where would we all be if it was not for me? I see Dodir Nade as a place where we exercise mercy towards one another. By God's grace, we are all here... But please be merciful to me, because I confess my attitude towards Serbs has been wrong in the past.*

(Teodora) *Yes, and my attitude towards Croats was wrong. I am guilty of falling into the trap of seeing the other side just as an enemy, and I have discriminated against the other.*

(Amina) *When I think about what happened in the war in my country, I find it hard to think about mercy. Yet I was inspired by the story of Jo and Pat. There has to be a place for mercy. Something has to break the cycle of violence and that is where mercy is crucial because it represents a new beginning.*

Narrator *So who do you fear?*

Mercy *I fear Justice.*

Justice (Comes forward. Sajra is wearing a symbol of scales. Rising to her feet and smiling, she bellows) *I stand with you Truth in exposing what has happened and my task is to make sure that something is done to repair the damage wreaked on innocent people. I am concerned about making things right. I look beneath the surface and behind the issues about which people seem to fight. I am aware that there seem to be different truths for each side of the war, Serb and Croat. These truths are the result of different histories and ways of interpreting events. Like Truth, I am like a torch shining light on the things that have been done. People must be held accountable for their actions.*

Truth *Life often is unfair especially when we think of the many evil things that were done in the name of a particular identity.*

Justice *What do you mean?*

Truth *Only a small number of people who are responsible for war-crimes are caught and brought to justice. What about the many*

In spite of our differences

people who colluded with the major players? Will the truth ever come out with all who were involved?

Narrator *Whom do you fear?*

Justice *I fear Peace.*

Peace (Aleksandra, wearing a symbol of a dove, smiling, steps forward) *We need safe spaces within which we can all feel safe to seek the truth about the atrocities that happened and why they happened. I hold the community together, with underlying respect for one another. We need more programmes like Dodir Nade where we all agree to listen and hear one another speak and listen to the voices of Truth, Mercy and Justice. I support Justice, Truth and Mercy because in order to have a lasting peace we need to hear your voices. One of our basic rules of meeting together is that we listen to one another.*

Justice *I used to think that when people talked about reconciliation, Justice was left out, but I am glad that I am regarded as an important part of this discussion.*

Mercy *Does a person want to live in a reconciling way? That is a crucial question for me. When the workshop has finished and we return home, how do we prepare the ground for reconciliation to take place? Who is responsible for doing that?*

Peace *Let us remember what we have been learning about in our activities together. Our second session was all about non-violent communication and how to deal with conflict. I feel that the way we deal with conflict is key. It is important not to avoid conflict but to see it as a means of learning about ourselves and one another. It can be a means of insight and connection. Non-Violent communication can help us all work with conflict in a non-threatening way. We must teach our children to be able to deal with conflict in non-violent ways.*

Justice *There have been so many atrocities in our region, not only recently, but also in World War 2. Truth is so evasive, one side will say the truth is with them and the other side will say the same, so what is the truth? The whole truth of what happened at Srebrenica will never be known, although bits and pieces emerge from time to time. There were so many crimes in our war. We shall never know what exactly happened. How do we arrive at the truth?*

Living in a reconciling way

Truth *The problem is that those who committed crimes are protected and people lie so that the truth never comes out. We need a Truth and Reconciliation Commission like they had in South Africa. But can we get agreement from all sides to do that? I feel that there is a lot of collusion in our government with those who committed atrocities.*

Justice *The search for Justice is long and complicated for many people but we must not give up, people must be accountable for their crimes. But will our governments help us bring the culprits to justice?*

Postcards for peace

Milena invites a person from each group to pick out a postcard which represents the theme of the group.

Viktoria chooses for Peace.

I work with small children in Čepin. I choose this English seaside view of families playing together on the beach. It reminds me of a lovely vision of peace, everyone enjoying the sunshine and being together. But it also reminds me of the fact that for many people in the world, even in England. a holiday is a luxury. We live in an unequal world.

Sajra, for Justice.

I choose a picture of the Black Forest in Germany and it reminds me of Justice and how we need to sow seeds of justice. The trees give shelter to the birds. We need to protect people from injustice. But it also reminds me of the need to include the whole of creation in our vision of Justice.

Lana, for Truth, chooses a picture of the Vatican in Rome.

I am thinking here of the Catholic Church and it is an imposing building. But we must also remember that other churches are just as important, Orthodox and Protestant, and the Methodist Church. But more important Sajra and Amina have reminded us to be open to what Islam can teach us.

Mario for Mercy.

I choose a picture of the Frauenkirche, (The Church of our Lady) in Dresden, which was bombed in 1945 by allied forces. The rebuilding of the church consists of 45% of the original stone material. *Although the British showed no mercy when they bombed Dresden, the new has arisen out of the old. The church has a Cross of nails from Coventry and there is now a close connection with Coventry Cathedral.*

Milena steps forward and says:

The picture of the Frauenkirche is a good place to end our conversation today. Let us all go forward in a spirit of rebuilding our relationships, taking the good from the past and reaching out to the future in hope.

Representatives from each group all join hands and invite the rest of the group to join them.

The Rainbow People

On the last morning, as we came to the end of our activities, we focused on what participants could do in their local communities for peace and reconciliation. To help this, the group acted out a short sketch, 'The Rainbow People'.[21]

The plot was very simple, reminding us of the story of creation and The Fall in the book of Genesis. In the beginning, a wind blew over the land warming people with life and love. As they explored their world they found different coloured ribbons, blue, green, red and yellow, which gave them great happiness. Another wind blew and they realised they were all different. They retreated into groups according to colour. They were isolated from each other and the feeling of warmth they had for one another had gone. Each of the four groups lacked something the others had.

Suddenly a stranger appeared and challenged them to end their isolation and give to each other what they need to be friends again. This they did. The coloured ribbons merged to form a beautiful rainbow.

Who was the stranger? We are not told. The stranger has a key role in being the catalyst for the group coming back together and rediscovering the joys of cooperating.

Mario mentioned the role of the stranger as an outsider giving aid and assistance. Knowing the history of the Centre for Peace, Non-violence and Human Rights in Osijek, he recalled the important role of outsiders in the early days of the Centre, and how

---

[21] Caroline Askar *The Rainbow People*

Living in a reconciling way

Adam Curle from the UK in particular was an important mentor, along with Bradford University Peace Studies Department.

In the discussion after the play, each person identified what they would do back home to live in a reconciling way. Amina and Sajra mentioned how they would assist the ongoing investigations into war crimes, not only in Bosnia but also in Croatia and Kosovo.

We need to document the crimes and bring people to justice.

Filip wanted to work with war veterans and support them and their families.

Lana was committed to working with young people and teaching them non-violent communication.

I want to get hold of the jackal and giraffe puppets.

Ivana was concerned about the families she had hurt through her anti-Serb activities and wanted to seek their forgiveness.

Every member of the group warmed to the invitation to train as a facilitator to lead Dodir Nade activities in their own communities.

Time was running out fast. There was still the Line of Health to re-enact. A line was quickly formed outside in the grounds, and members of the group positioned themselves on a scale of 1 to 10. Judith and I were keen to see the positions. Had any changed? What was the difference between now and the start?

Lana began the conversation by saying her score had gone down to 5 from 8.

To be seen as strong by the young people I work with, I gave myself a high score before. I was not being honest with myself and with you.

The biggest difference was with Filip.

Thanks to playing the paralysed man, I place myself at 7. I feel so different about myself. I have wounds still and I have flashbacks because of the war. But after that healing experience in the first session, I feel more in control of my situation and I am not so paralysed. I just need to control the alcohol.

Everyone else was more or less the same, though giving themselves slightly higher scores.

As this was the last session, several members of the group were asking for prayer for healing. It was on the plan for the day

In spite of our differences

anyway, but I was struck by their insistence that we make time for healing prayer. My focus was the account of Peter getting out of the boat in response to Jesus bidding him to walk on the water, as told by Matthew 14:22-32. I made the link with members of the group 'getting out of the boat' and moving out of their comfort zone to attend the Dodir Nade sessions. Living in a reconciling way would involve more challenges, more getting out of the boat. They would need to exercise trust in themselves and in one another if they were to be channels of peace in their own communities.

The session was coming to a close. It is customary for each person to receive a certificate for attending the course. These are given out randomly and they in turn hand the certificate to the correct person. As they do this, they add a word of encouragement, accompanied by a hug, a kiss and tears.

For the team, we had come to the end of a long journey together. The goodbyes, photos and the hugs lasted a long time. Now they all got into their cars and headed for home. Nena and Snježana dropped Judith and me at the station outside the village where we waited for our train to Zagreb. The quietness of the station contrasted with the hubbub of the workshop. The silence before the train arrived was wonderful. It was, however, soon broken when the train pulled into the station. The old blue and white carriages were full of students returning to the capital after the weekend. They talk to us eagerly, in perfect English.

'So, what brings you to Croatia?' they asked. *'Da su moji prijatelji duga priča.'* (That, my friends, is a long story).

Chapter 15

A call within a call

> *But there are deep sicknesses and diseases from which contemporary man is suffering and much of our therapy is only a treatment of its symptoms. Only a deep ministry can touch the hurts that a war-torn century has inflicted on the inner being of man.*[22]

It is the deep ministry, which touches the hurts, to which I am called. I remember using the word 'called' at school when I was asked by the career's teacher about my plans for the future. At 19 years of age, I told him, I felt called to be a psychiatric social worker. The career's teacher looked at me quizzically. 'In an interview,' he said, 'do not use the word 'call'. If you do, the panel will just think you are mentally unstable'. Yet in the church the word 'call' is often used. We talk about a 'call to ministry.' Mine – to be a Methodist minister – was tested by the church. I was accepted for training and ordained as a minister in 1983. The testing process was very rigorous. However, within this call to ordained ministry, I became aware of a deeper call to be engaged in reconciliation work.

In Milton Keynes, I remember asking the Christian Council to support the setting up of a link between the churches in Milton Keynes and an ecumenical area in Leipzig, in the former German Democratic Republic. I emphasised the importance of reconciliation between East and West Europe. A minister rose to his feet and said: 'It is all very well making these links but the important task for the Church is to preach the Gospel.' I stood up and said my understanding of the Gospel was that reconciliation was at the heart of our faith. When I first came into contact with the Centre for Peace, Non-Violence and Human Rights in Osijek, I saw its work as being an integral part of the 'new thing' God was doing out of the chaos and despair of the war. I wanted to support its inspiring work.

Twenty-four years have now passed since the consultation in 2001 when our work with Bench We Share evolved into Dodir

---

[22] *The Christian Healing Ministry* p143 Morris Maddocks

In spite of our differences

Nade. Over these years, we developed a pattern of workshops in Croatia, Serbia and Bosnia and Herzegovina. An important new part of our work is to equip people to run workshops in their own communities. The work has had a significant effect upon who I am. If I were to complete the mask exercise in the session on identity now, compared with 25 years ago, it would be markedly different for me.

I remained in the Leamington Spa Circuit until 2007. My time there was very rewarding. Mediation and Community Support was founded and I gained experience in delivering training and providing conflict support and mediation to neighbours, churches and in the workplace. However, I was in turmoil, experiencing the burden of a call to devote more time to the work of Dodir Nade. On one hand I felt fulfilled working in Leamington Spa, but on the other, I was being drawn very clearly into the work in Croatia. The workshops we delivered in Croatia were receiving good feedback. Participants were testifying to the healing and fresh energy they received to work for peace in their own communities. I could see the potential for holding more workshops and extending the work to other parts of Croatia, Bosnia and Herzegovina, Kosovo, Serbia and Macedonia. Whenever I returned home after a visit to the region, it took at least a week before I could totally reintegrate myself back into the routine of Methodist meetings and taking services. It was difficult managing the transition. From leading sessions in Croatia dealing with the hurts of the war in a workshop, two days later I'd be holding church councils dealing with everyday concerns of the local church.

Help was at hand in my vocational crisis. Penny, a member of the Society of Friends, became my mentor. I was invited to speak at a conference in Shropshire about Dodir Nade. Penny discerned I was struggling, torn between working within the structures of the Methodist system as a minister, and following God's call to develop peace and reconciliation work. I shared with her how I came alive when I was doing the work of Touch of Hope, but how frustrated I was at times with church work. I had a call within a call. I was mindful of what Ray Davey at the Corrymeela Community told people as they left the Community after a workshop.

'Remember that Corrymeela begins when you arrive at home.'

A call within a call

I told myself that if change was going to happen, it needed change at the local level, in local churches and communities. The Methodist people were so supportive of the work and I was receiving Methodist money both nationally and from local groups.

My Superintendent also sensed my struggle. He suggested I should apply to the Methodist Church to be a Mission Partner in the former Yugoslavia, while remaining in the UK as a minister in pastoral charge of churches. Mission Partners are attached to Methodist Churches overseas for specific duties in the country concerned. Subsequent discussions and negotiations within the World Church Office and the Methodist Church in Serbia went round and round in circles and led to me being even more frustrated. I valued the support of Penny all the more as I jumped through the various hoops in applying to be a Mission Partner. The European Affairs Secretary of the Methodist Church at the time fully supported my application.

There were several issues involved. First, Mission Partners work with Methodist churches and I was not working with a church in Croatia. I was working with a secular organisation, namely the Centre for Peace, Non-Violence and Human Rights in Osijek. Later on, when our workers Nena and Snježana left the Centre for Peace, the Nansen Dialogue Centre in Osijek became our administrative base. There is no Methodist Church in Croatia. There are however, Methodist Churches in Serbia and Macedonia, but at that stage, I had not made contact with them. We work with people of faith, all faiths and no faith. The religious make up of Croatia is around 90% Roman Catholic and 5% Serbian Orthodox, with a small percentage of other Christian groups such as Baptist, Pentecostal and Seventh Day Adventist. There is also a small number of members of the Islamic Faith. Secondly, Mission Partners are based wholly overseas, so the idea of me being based in the UK, though a good one from my point of view, was really a non-starter. Thirdly, I was informed by a member of the World Church team that I was a 'problem'. When men and women applied to the Methodist Church to be a Mission Partner, the Church decided where a person should work. They were not used to people like me who knew exactly where they should be. The World Church office offered me the possibility of working in Sri Lanka, but I felt very firmly my place was in Croatia. I was different from other applicants because I was already working in Croatia and felt called to work on the issue of Reconciliation.

Therefore, it was with much reluctance, that when the time came to leave Leamington Spa, I was sent to Rugby as Superintendent of the Rugby and Daventry circuit in 2007. I was very happy in this new circuit and settled in quickly. I was keen to establish the work of the Mediation service in Rugby, which led to Judith and me becoming part of the Anti-Social Behaviour Management meetings with Rugby Borough Council. We took on cases for neighbourhood disputes and ran training courses for new mediators.

My burden intensified in Rugby. I became more and more stressed from trying to express my vocation with Dodir Nade alongside the mediation work locally. Having been called into the peace work, I felt sure the time would come when I would be able to devote more time to it. However, I had to wait. I thought about the words of Jesus in John 2:4 *My hour has not yet come*. This is in response to the mother of Jesus asking him to intervene at the wedding when the wine had run out. I was acutely aware of the distinction between Kronos, chronological time and Kairos, the right time or the appointed time. The right time had not come yet. I had waited a very long time, but I had to wait just a little longer. I shared all of this with Penny and also my colleague Deacon Janet Thomas. With her encouragement, I decided to push doors and explore working half time in the Rugby Circuit. I shared with the Circuit Stewards how I felt a deep inner call to develop the peace work. However, I felt committed to being a minister within the circuit. I decided to apply once more to the appropriate committee in the Methodist Church. Once again, I attended a special committee arranged for ministers feeling called to work outside the local church framework. I had to prepare a statement detailing my call to the work. Looking back, the hardest act for me was to tell my church, Rugby Methodist Church Centre, I was called to devote more time to the peace work. The church had expected me to stay for at least five years. I felt I was letting them down at having to curtail my appointment as Superintendent. My ministerial colleague was asked if he would take over. To my relief, he accepted.

A call within a call

The result was excellent – at last everything seemed to fit. I was granted permission to work half time in the Circuit and half as a Conflict Resolution Practitioner with Dodir Nade. The timing was at last right. The hour had come.

A retired minister and his wife volunteered to raise the necessary money to allow this to happen. Through their efforts, a Methodist Church grant, half a stipend plus money from donors pledging money each month, it was possible.

From September 2011, I was no longer Superintendent. My responsibility switched to the Methodist churches in Long Lawford and Lutterworth. Now, working half-time with Dodir Nade, I could not believe that at last it was to happen. Once again, the support of Penny and my mediation colleague Judith were invaluable.

Long Lawford is a small village just outside Rugby. The chapel membership had declined to just single figures. However, I felt the church had a future because there were many green shoots, particularly as a result of a young people's worker. To close the chapel would be like pouring weed killer over those shoots. A vibrant mums and toddlers' group had been formed and there was a lively youth club. Anti-social behaviour from young people was rife in the community and the youth club was a welcome addition to the village. The chapel was making a significant contribution to the community. My time at Long Lawford was very happy. Likewise, I was also very satisfied at Lutterworth. A big need in the community was to support the carers of people living with dementia. A church member worked professionally in the sector, so with her guidance the church started a group for carers which met a real need. All worked out well at these churches and I value my time there because we were fulfilling our calling as churches.

Reflecting on my journey with the church at this time, Penny recalled our first meeting at the conference in Shropshire, where, she says, I was spinning on my own axis from lack of focus, my energy dispersed, trying to cope with the demands of home and church, being pushed and pulled in lots of directions. She noticed a marked change in me after I began working half time in the local church. She felt it was the first time the Methodist Church nationally had really heard me express the call. With Penny's help, I started to organise a mountain of paperwork I had accumulated over the years to do with the peace work. I moved from a position of inner turmoil to fulfilling my calling. She likens this change to the constant rising of the phoenix in the way that I had the clarity to be assertive and not be pushed around by others. To use an image from Greek mythology, I rose like a phoenix from the ashes and emerged a much stronger person after the trial.

To mark my change in status, a committee was appointed by Community for Reconciliation to oversee the day to day running of the work.

It also enabled the work to extend geographically – to Serbia and Bosnia and Herzegovina – and start training facilitators to work in their own communities.

Chapter 16

Sitting together on the bench in the UK

'Is Croatia in East or West Africa?' she asked. 'I can't remember.'

I remember going to a post office in Birmingham to post a package to Croatia and being asked this question.

At that time, Croatia and Bosnia were constantly in the news, making her question hard to swallow. It highlighted an issue I encounter regularly when asked to speak about the work of Dodir Nade. Where exactly are Croatia, Serbia and Bosnia and Herzegovina? I always start by showing maps of Europe and the former Yugoslavia, so people will know where the work is based. However, it is not just the geography which is an issue. They are often confused about who was fighting whom in the conflict. For example, after giving talks about Croatia, the person giving the vote of thanks will say something like, 'well thank you Clive for the talk about Kosovo.' People mix up the countries, confused about the causes of the conflict. I have some sympathy with this, because I too was confused, even disorientated, when I first set foot in Croatia in 1996.

Study visits to the UK

At the beginning of my involvement with Bench We Share, the original suggestion to bring a group over to England was a throwaway line. At the time I did not expect Dušanka to take up the offer. From the perspective of groups coming from the region, a study visit to the UK is not a sightseeing trip. Rather, it contributes to the overall aim of the programme in healing the hurts of war.

The pattern of the visits to the UK has not changed since that first visit in April 1997. A visit lasts from seven to ten days and always includes an intensive residential experience for three days which, apart from one visit, has always been at Barnes Close, the residential centre for Community for Reconciliation. The residential setting is the ideal opportunity to do some intensive work together. A visit to Coventry Cathedral is included. This involves a guided tour around the Cathedral and a chance to discuss things with Cathedral staff. In the participants' evaluations

In spite of our differences

of the visit to the UK, the visit to Coventry Cathedral is highly regarded. The symbolism of the new emerging from the ruins of the old is very rich and speaks of death and resurrection. The Coventry story of reconciliation impresses and challenges groups on Dodir Nade visits.

Group members stay with church families, whose generous hospitality gives a very powerful message of unconditional acceptance. Hosts are generally members of churches and our visitors attend services with their hosts. The visitors are invited to speak at church about themselves, their experience of the war and how Dodir Nade has helped them in their journey of reconciliation. Attending churches, which are mostly Methodist, is for many a new experience, especially as some participants come from the Serbian Orthodox Church tradition, where the pattern and style of worship is totally different from the Methodist hymn-sandwich. Our guests often comment on the quality of the ecumenical work in the churches. As a committed ecumenist, I often feel depressed about the state of ecumenism in the UK, but it is heartening to hear from our visitors how impressed they are with inter-church relations here.

We always have an open public meeting for our visitors, with an opportunity for them to share their stories. Hearing their experience of the war is always a very moving experience. As noted in the first visit to the UK, the open meeting at Lyndon church was a very emotional time. You could hear a pin drop as group members shared their experiences. Participants can be very emotional, and the reality of the suffering caused by war is plain for all to see.

Visitors come if they have completed the six workshops in our programme. The UK study visit is now the bridging session between the initial workshops and being training to lead workshops. By immersing in another country and culture, we hope the experience will enhance their own work for reconciliation as they compare and contrast how we work, or don't work, for reconciliation in the UK.

Particularly in the early days of our work, the situation in Croatia was often described as being sterile. The UK visit offers people the chance to come away from the stress of living in the region and the chance to relax in the company of like-minded people. We hope the participants will be refreshed, inwardly and outwardly, from their time with us. The experience of people from different sides of the conflict, travelling together in one group, is very therapeutic in itself. Much healing takes place, not in the actual workshops but informally being together.

Dušanka coined the phrase 'spontaneous impartial mediator' in relation to my role when working with Bench We Share in Croatia. Similarly, the people whom our visitors meet take on this role in the questions they ask about the work of the programme. Participants open up to almost complete strangers when asked about what happened in the war. When our guests share their experiences there is a cathartic effect, which encourages ongoing healing.

From the perspective of those in the UK, what are the important aspects of having these visits? I have already made the point about the importance of geography of the region. The visits help church members and others to think and pray more intelligently about the situation in post-war Croatia, Serbia and Bosnia and Herzegovina.

The second important message is that ordinary people are making a difference to their communities, using non-violent methods of resolving conflict. I recall Katarina Kruhonja's words:

The beginning of my personal dedication to peace work and reconciliation could be placed in the moment when I became aware of my part of responsibility for what was going on – it was in summer 1991. I became aware that my own passivity towards politics was a factor which also contributed to outbreak of the war.

What inspires me is that men and women are following Katarina's example and taking responsibility for tackling violence in their communities. I hope men and women in the UK will be inspired to use non-violent methods in tackling issues of violence in the UK. When our visitors give presentations about their experience of workshops, people in the audience often comment they have never thought at all about the issues of post-war reconstruction and the rebuilding of trust in communities.

There is also a funding aspect to this. Once the Balkans fell out of the headlines, it became more difficult to raise money for our work. The area is no longer seen to be in need of assistance. Croatia

In spite of our differences

is a top holiday destination and is a member of the EU. People question the need for our work. We only see footage of the conflict in ex-Yugoslavia on our TV screens when a high-profile war criminal is in the news. Then people are reminded of the war in the '90s and can appreciate the need for our work. When participants share their wartime experiences in churches, credibility is given to our work. People can see the difference the workshops have made to individuals.

It is important for people here to realise the complexity of the causes of the disintegration of Yugoslavia. One irritating comment I hear often is,

If only they believed in the Lord Jesus Christ and were saved, they would not be feeling as they do, and there would be a lot more peace in the world.

I explain many of our participants are active believers, but that does not mean they are not hurting. They are seeking answers and struggling inwardly with the effects of loss and trauma. Some participants have lost their faith and others describe themselves as atheist or agnostic. At one presentation, I was speaking about some of the issues people were experiencing in Vukovar. A woman, well-spoken and smartly dressed, told the meeting she had been to Vukovar on a Danube cruise. She had gone into a pub and seen men sitting around drinking and smoking.

After World War 2, British people did not sit around drinking and smoking cigarettes but started to rebuild their country. Why don't those men in Vukovar do the same?

I tried to answer her, but she seemed convinced by her own arguments. First, I asked her what she had observed. She realised she had been making assumptions about the situation. I explained the problems men and women face in securing meaningful employment in Vukovar. Secondly, I talked about the difficulties many people face raising finance for new business ventures. It is hard to make comparisons with the UK, given that our histories and circumstances are totally different. When we do have visitors from the region, they are able to explain their situation far better than I can. People then realise the complexity of the situation.

A large proportion of our money comes from individual donations within the Methodist Church and grants from the

Sitting together on the bench in the UK

Methodist Church itself. When people attend the open meetings and listen to our guests, they can hear and see how the money is spent. Talks by our guests are a means of fund-raising. However, the majority of our funding has come through the Methodist Church, through the generous giving of members, coffee mornings and the Methodist Fund for World Mission.

Participants who have been to the UK are more inclined to complete our training in facilitation and go on to work in their own communities for peace and reconciliation. Friendships have been formed between hosts and their guests that have continued over the years. The most felicitous friendship has been that formed between Margaret and Katarina, who stayed with Margaret on the very first visit to Birmingham. The way their friendship developed into the work of supporting children and young people in Baranja is an outstanding example of what can happen when we open our homes to a guest.

We have also created school links. One such link was with a local primary school near Lutterworth in Bitteswell, St Mary's C of E Primary School. I took a school assembly about peace and talked about Bench We Share. This assembly went down very well, which led to me leading a session in a school class focussing on the work we do in Croatia. The teachers asked if the children could link with a school in Osijek. Through Snježana, I made contact with a primary school in Osijek and its English teacher. I was delighted when children of both schools exchanged letters. I was very impressed with the standard of English in the letters from Osijek. The next stage was for a group from Croatia to visit the school, with the children providing hospitality. Nena spoke in assembly and visited classes. She even taught the children some games.

The current Head Teacher, Hayley Cupit writes:

I remember this time well – it was a lovely connection to forge and the children and staff thoroughly enjoyed communicating with the children from Croatia. I remember it was a lovely day when Nena came in – the children served them tea, as I remember, and we all chatted. The games were great fun and the assembly was very informative for the children, which gave them the chance to show empathy and gratitude for the lives they lead, while thinking of others who were less fortunate than themselves. It

In spite of our differences

made this real to them, as often it is difficult to open the children's eyes to the world we live in when they live in their little Bitteswell Bubble.

The most recent visit to a Junior and Infant school in Nuneaton was by the combined Croatian/Bosnian group. These visits to schools give the groups a fascinating insight into English schools. In group evaluations, the school visits usually have a high rating. Such links are important to improve mutual understanding across borders. It is also an opportunity to talk about peace issues. Over the years, I have spoken in many schools about the work and I have wanted to link talking about the work with Peace Education, but sadly this has not happened. School links require a lot of hard work and commitment if they are to be successful. The constraints of the national curriculum also make it difficult to maintain the links.

Chapter 17

Channels of healing

After the frosty encounter at Belgrade airport, Judith and I travelled to Novi Sad to be with a group of participants whose workshop was being led by newly trained facilitators. It was being held at the premises of Ecumenical Humanitarian Organisation (EHO) whose address is Cirila I Metodija 21.[23] We were welcomed warmly by Marija Parnicky, a Slovakian, who attends the Methodist Church in the predominantly Slovakian settlement of Kisač, near Novi Sad. EHO is a major non-governmental organisation (NGO) in Vojvodina, engaged in humanitarian work locally. We are grateful to Maria because she has opened many doors for Dodir Nade. She is experienced in active non-violence training, conflict resolution, peace building and human rights. She is very active in coordinating women's work ecumenically in Serbia, and has a lot of contacts across Central and Eastern Europe. Maria knows Nena well, having worked with her on different projects. The work of Dodir Nade has developed in a major way through our partnership with Maria. She remains a valued and trusted contact in Serbia.

Our three facilitators were in a state of panic. Mario, Amina and Lana were busy working out who was going to do what. They said they were feeling very unprepared. They recalled Judith's words about the importance of planning a workshop in detail, where each leader has an aide-memoire of the qualities of a facilitator.

A good facilitator is knowledgeable about their subject, organised, well prepared, able to listen, asks the right questions, non-judgemental, impartial, respectful of all people, knows their own limitations, seeks to know themselves, willing to learn from mistakes.

---

[23] Cyril and Methodius went as missionaries to Russia. They also translated the Gospels into the Slavic tongue. Cyril devised an alphabet, which is still used in Russia and in other Slavic countries.

In spite of our differences

The first session was to be on Health and Healing, Amina taking the lead in asking people to draw a picture of what a healthy person looks like.

The group arrived, 12 people of mixed nationality, age and gender. The atmosphere was convivial as they helped themselves to drinks and snacks. The group included caring agency workers, church workers, students, a psychologist, war veterans and a retired teacher. Judith and I were delighted the group was so mixed. The participants had been encouraged to attend by Marija and past participants.

Our three facilitators called the group to order and then invited each person to introduce themselves. They ran through the preliminaries of the ground rules and the order of the day. The team was confident and enthusiastic as they commenced the first task. Three groups formed and each drew a picture of what a healthy person looks like. The morning passed quickly. The group was lively and communicative, describing their pictures, defining health and evaluating their own. However, the leaders ran into difficulty in drawing out the discussion. They fell into the trap of thinking they had to supply the answers, instead of enabling the participants to speak. The team floundered when the discussion dried up and looked longingly at Judith, Nena and me for guidance. I had noticed our trainees could lead activities very well, but had difficulty following through a discussion, not knowing what to do or say. It is one thing knowing what an activity entails and another knowing its purpose. This comes with experience.

After lunch, issues arose for the team over the story and ensuing discussion of the healing of the paralysed man. Mario asked the group in what ways were they paralysed in the community. The paralysed man, played by Stjepan, a Croat, talked about his own trauma as a war veteran, saying how paralysed he was, emotionally, physically and spiritually, because of the war. He had been a young man when he enlisted into the army. He'd had dreams of going to university then into business. The experience of seeing so many people wounded and killed had left a profound impression on him. He had lost confidence in himself and could not see any point in living. Both Amina and Mario found it hard to respond to him for different reasons. Amina was taken back to her time in Bosnia and began to have flashbacks of atrocities. Mario related well to him, but wanted desperately to share his faith. He admitted to his former dislike of Serbs and Serbia. Stjepan found the journey from Osijek challenging as he crossed the border at Ilok. Mario found himself wanting to share his own experience of previously hating Serbs and how he had overcome that. Lana came to Amina and Mario's rescue. As she had had a completely different experience of the war, she was able to listen carefully to Stjepan. Somehow, he felt satisfied and relieved he had been able to share his feelings. This is the beauty of having a team of workers who can share the load of leading the activities.

It was important Judith, Nena and I spent time with the team reflecting on what had happened.

The experience with Mario and Amina emphasised that all facilitators, including me, have our own red flags and blind spots when it comes to leading sessions. Sometimes somebody in the group may say or do something that reminds one of a previous difficult or painful experience. Our new facilitators have varied experiences of the war and some will have experience of what happened in Vukovar. Some facilitators have lost family or property in the war and will have negative feelings about people with whom they were and are in conflict. Mario realised there was much he had not worked through. He was grateful the session had exposed his vulnerability. As facilitators we seek to be non-judgmental and impartial, but this is a challenge for our new workers. Hence a big part of the preparation is for facilitators to be as self-aware as possible and learn how to deal with those difficult moments. We work in teams, so we can monitor each other's way of working, lest we fall into the traps of being partial and judgemental. Critical debriefing after leading a session is essential to improve our practice as workers.

Considering all these facilitators had been through personally and that this was their first experience of leading, we were very satisfied with how they led the session.

From the beginning of the work, my fellow committee members were asking when Dodir Nade was going to begin training the trainers. For a long time, I did not feel the time was right as it was too close in time to the fighting, too early in the programme. A big breakthrough came when Nena secured help from a regional fund, the Ecumenical Women's Initiative. Nena put together a Facilitation Skills manual and met with Judith and me to add input. We used material from our mediation work in the UK, particularly our values, principles and various exercises to do with active listening.

Judith brings her particular skills and resources as a trainer to this particular part of our work. She has had years of experience delivering training and is very creative in her thinking in meeting the needs of the trainees. We held sessions for small numbers of people and slowly built up our curriculum. A growing number of helpers, who had been through the programme, were joining us in sessions and helping in many different ways, organising the flipchart, running the games, assisting with translation. This was in keeping with our goal of empowering men and women to be channels of healing in their own communities. This greatly enhanced our working together, as those who helped were an encouragement to new participants who struggled with some of the themes.

It is a huge step forward for Dodir Nade, that finally we have put together a course to equip people to run sessions in their own communities. It is the most exciting part of our current work and we are greatly encouraged by seeing how former participants are so readily thinking about carrying on the work. It is a big priority to train more facilitators so that the work will grow.

Here are two examples of participants. Rahela, a Croat, attended workshops many years ago. She left us for a while to start a family and then came back, helping out with translation and running activities. She completed the facilitation skills training and works in her local church with young people on non-violent communication.

Milijana, a Serb from Borovo, led a session on Eating Healthily. Judith, Nena and I attended. The choice of theme has a lot to do with her own personal wounds. She had two sons, the younger was a conscript in the army and she had not known whether he was alive or dead for three months. Unfortunately, tragedy struck when her elder son Bobo died in a car accident. Emotionally devastated, she and her husband Nenad put on weight. On one occasion they had guests from Bosnia who appeared to look so healthy. From then onwards, she committed to eating more healthily, completed a course in healthy cooking and started to teach children to eat healthily. She was attracted to Dodir Nade because she had heard she could explore health and healing. For her, the most difficult topic was forgiveness. After the meetings, the participants were not enemies any more but friends, treating each other differently. Milijana had always wanted to be a teacher but was denied the opportunity as a young person. She found fulfilment teaching children to eat healthily and leapt at the chance to be a facilitator.

Milijana invited six people of differing nationalities, including Aleksandra, to her session. Each brought ingredients; rice, vegetables, fruit, flour, to cook a meal together. Milijana is a gentle, gracious person who allotted jobs to the group and together they prepared a tasty meal of vegetable risotto, salads and fruit pies. Over the meal we laughed and joked. People soon relaxed enough to express their anxieties and support each other. I was impressed with how Milijana led the session so competently, how she listened with undivided attention to people's concerns. Each of the participants had experienced personal tragedy, losing loved ones and, in some cases, property as well. As each shared their story, we all shed tears and Milijana was sensitive to people's feelings. She is a good example of someone who was empowered to lead.

Chapter 18

Affirmation and a surprise meeting in Osijek

Krunoslav-Sukić Award

In autumn 2014, 18 years after I first set foot in Osijek, Nena informed me that I had been nominated to receive the Krunoslav-Sukić award. This award is in memory of Kruno, one of the founders of the Centre for Peace, Non-Violence and Human Rights in Osijek. The recognition is awarded to people, initiatives, schools and organisations whose work contributes to the protection and promotion of human rights and promotes a culture of peace and non-violence. After several nail-biting weeks, I was informed the nomination was successful and I received the award on 14 December 2014. The ceremony was held in the National Theatre building in Osijek, which dates back to the Austro-Hungarian empire of the 19th century. I received a large certificate for my involvement with Bench We Share and Dodir Nade. The presentation was a huge affirmation of the work since 1996. After all the ups and downs of the early years and the struggle for funding, I was thankful for the recognition Dodir Nade had received. I had to give a short speech and I recalled the words of Katarina Kruhonja.

The beginning of my personal dedication to peace work and reconciliation could be placed in the moment when I became aware of my part of responsibility for what was going on – it was in summer 1991. I became aware that my own passivity towards politics was a factor which also contributed to outbreak of the war.

The words continue to inspire me not to complain about the violence in my own community and the wider world. On the contrary, we must tackle the violence through non-violent means. I was determined not just to be part of the problem, but to be part of the answer. I believe I was the first person from the UK to be given the award. I could not believe it and it felt very humbling to be there alongside others also receiving awards. The citation acknowledged my work with East Germany and as a mediator

Affirmation and a surprise meeting in Osijek

with Mediation and Community Support. The words of a former participant from Dodir Nade were quoted.

I have gained more confidence, peace and begun my own spiritual development for the possibility of reconciliation and forgiveness, that I'm trying to share now with my loved ones, organisation and in my community.

Two years later, there was a surprise email from the British Ambassador to Croatia. At first, I could not believe the words. The Ambassador was inviting me to meet Prince Charles in Osijek. The Prince of Wales was touring the Balkans and planned to spend 23 March 2016 at a peace event. Subsequently, I met Prince Charles along with an ecumenical group of Church leaders and the local Imam, who had been hastily brought together. We had to wait some time before the prince arrived and we attempted to have a discussion about the role of faith communities in the aftermath of the fighting, but the discussion was very strained. It seemed strange that I should travel all the way to Osijek to meet a member of the royal family. On being introduced as a Methodist minister, Prince Charles said:

You can always rely on the Methodists to be doing good things.

In 2025, where are we with the work of Dodir Nade?

When the pandemic came in 2020, sadly we had to suspend all our work. At last, in spring 2022 we were able to travel to Osijek to assess the ongoing need. We had planned to work with Croatian war veterans but, alas, the group had been unable to meet during the pandemic and was in disarray. Our local worker Snježana, however, put together a group of 12 people including war veterans and others in Tenja, a small village outside Osijek and we held a taster workshop. Three thousand people from Tenja were displaced from their homes in 1991, and between 1996 and 1998 Tenja was under the control of United Nations Transitional Administration for Eastern Slavonia (UNTAES).

We visited past participants in Vukovar and discovered the water tower has been restored. The former restaurant in the tower is now a permanent exhibition, chronicling the fall of Vukovar. The town itself, together with Osijek, is a popular stopping off place for cruise ships plying up and down the Danube.

In spite of our differences

The other significant event on this visit was the launch of a book by peace activist Dragica Aleksa. Dragica attended Touch of Hope workshops and is well known in the Osijek area for her interreligious dialogue work and commitment to ecumenism. The event was attended by many peace activists and I was asked to bring greetings from the UK. What struck me was the assumption by local workers that Dodir Nade must continue its work as the need for our work is just as urgent as ever.

We followed our usual pattern of workshops. Two took place in Serbia, which did not go down too well with the therapist of one of our participants:

You cannot go there, that is where the enemy is.

Snježana formed a group with eight women (seven Croatian, one Serbian) who had been victims of sexual and physical violence in Serb camps in Croatia and Serbia. Two Croatian women (one visually impaired and the other originally from Bosnia). Four Serbian women from Serbia who were members of a women's group working for interreligious dialogue. Two men, one of whom was Croatian and visually impaired and the other originally from Bosnia. A Ukrainian couple from Kherson attended three workshops before leaving the region.

Each workshop included interactive activities, Biblical input and material from conflict resolution practice and non-violent communication. The prayer for healing became an important part of the sessions. The workshops provided a safe space for participants to share their hurts, frustrations, hopes and dreams. There were tears and laughter, heartache and joy in all the sessions.

For the final follow-up workshop, we concentrated on the theme of non-violent communication, acting out the story of Zacchaeus, trying to get behind his character to understand him. Was he such an evil person? We looked at the different kinds of communication expressed in the story – judgment, criticism, self-righteousness – comparing those with the way Jesus treated him. We asked the question: Who and where is Zacchaeus in our own community?

Future plans are to train facilitators to lead workshops in their own communities and to start a new cycle of workshops for a new group.

Affirmation and a surprise meeting in Osijek

The impact of Dodir Nade on my thinking about reconciliation

My experience of working with Dodir Nade has had a huge influence on my work as a person, mediator and Methodist minister. Writing these words, I realise they are a massive understatement. You will recall from what I wrote earlier, I was inspired by my first visit to Osijek in 1996 to set up a mediation service for neighbour disputes in the UK. Subsequently, Mediation and Community Support was set up. Despite setbacks in funding, the organisation has grown in its provision for training in conflict resolution and offering mediation and conflict coaching for people in dispute.

I first heard about non-violent communication in Osijek. It is an invaluable tool in working with conflict creatively. Non-violent communication enables people to stand back and connect with their feelings and needs, expressing empathy with oneself and others. We have introduced non-violent communication in our conflict resolution training.

Reflecting on the workshops, the conversation between Truth, Mercy, Justice and Peace has had a big impact on me. As mediators, Judith and I identify with the voices of Truth, Mercy, Justice and Peace, noting their presence in any conflict. In our mediation work there can be arguments about the truth, what exactly happened, when, where and how. Sometimes there will be the voice of mercy and a person may offer forgiveness, but only as long as the recipient fulfils a condition. There are calls for justice to be done. For example, in a neighbour dispute between two families, one neighbour may insist on local authority sanctions being imposed upon the other when that neighbour is perceived as being the guilty party. Peace is represented by how the structure of the mediation process works out in practice. There are ground rules for the joint meetings and a structure that allows everyone to have their say. The mediators are impartial and non-judgemental.

The road to justice is very slow in Croatia, Serbia, Kosovo and Bosnia and Herzegovina. Every day I receive a newsletter from the Balkan Investigative Reporting Network (BIRN) concerning Transitional Justice in the former Yugoslavia. The term Transitional Justice concerns the way countries deal with large-scale, systematic abuses of human rights. It recognises the dignity of individuals, the redress and acknowledgment of violations, with the aim of preventing the violations from happening again. BIRN's mission is to build sustainable peace, assisting healing and moving toward reconciliation. There is a seemingly endless stream of reports of trials and retrials of those who are accused of war-crimes. There are frequent references to events and crimes committed in places where Dodir Nade hold workshops, particularly the Vukovar area. In the UK, we hear little about trials and investigations into atrocities. In Croatia, Serbia and Bosnia and Herzegovina, there are continual references to the violence perpetrated. This makes it difficult for us to hold workshops in healing when the political mood can be antagonistic towards reconciliation. This situation is not helped by the fact that there are constantly political tensions in Kosovo with occasional outbursts of violence between Serbs and Kosovan Albanians. The region is still turbulent, exacerbated by the war in Ukraine. The need for our work is as urgent as ever.

Working with Dodir Nade has helped me be more informed about the nature of reconciliation. I love the quote from the former Archbishop of Canterbury, Rowan Williams: *Reconciliation is such a seductively comfortable word.*[24] Many people in churches seem to have a very cosy view of reconciliation, a superficial view that masks real differences, or injustice that has not been addressed. The word 'reconciliation' can roll easily off the tongue. I prefer to use the phrase 'living in a reconciling way.' Lederach's way of looking at reconciliation takes seriously the need to listen out for the voice of Justice alongside those of Truth, Mercy and Peace.

Men and women who attend Dodir Nade workshops are exploring living in a reconciling way. The very fact they want to be part of a mixed nationality group says a lot about their commitment. Despite opposition from peers, family members and professionals, they are prepared to attend the full programme of workshops. Repeatedly, participants will say how hard it was to attend their first workshop, how difficult it was to hear a person from the other side speak in Serbian or Croatian. Communication has emerged as being the most helpful workshop. Non-violent communication equips people to empathise with themselves, and with one another, with the aim of understanding each other's

---

[24] Rowan Williams *On Christian Theology* Blackwell Publishers 2000 p266 – quoted by David Stevens in *The Land of Unlikeness*

Affirmation and a surprise meeting in Osijek

perspective. They see each other as human beings. They listen to the voices of Truth, Mercy, Justice and Peace. For many of those who have been victims of rape, sexual violence and torture, there has been no justice. Few perpetrators are ever charged or brought to court. They live with the fact that their assailants are unlikely to face justice. For all the members of the groups, life is hard as they struggle with PTSD and painful memories. Yet they value the love and acceptance they experience from one another, despite being former enemies.

Identity has emerged as the most difficult workshop. The exercise in which we ask participants to say when their identity is hurt or threatened has proved particularly challenging. It has been no less challenging when we have used the Identity workshop material in a Birmingham junior school, working with teachers and children. Identity was often looked at in relation to the Black Lives Matter movement and race relations. I am convinced the material we use is relevant today in our own country, in matters of Equality, Diversity and Inclusion. In the mask exercise, an Asian teacher shared her painful experience of being discriminated against as a teacher, as she shared about times when her identity was hurt.

Similarly, in community and in churches, when we talk about Forgiveness and Reconciliation, Dodir Nade has so much to offer in providing a way of working with conflict creatively, a process that brings people together. There is a need for more work in healing the hurts between different groups of people that have been in conflict with one another.

A minister once approached me about a situation in his church. Several members from different parts of Eastern and Central Europe were in conflict. There were constant arguments and the unity of the church was under threat. The minister could not understand how, as Christians, they were so locked in conflict. When the minister heard about our work, he began to see how the different groups might be able to come together if given space to explore living in a reconciling way. The members in conflict were carrying baggage from the old Soviet empire and its hostilities between the member countries. They needed the space and time to listen to one another and explore living in a reconciling way.

In spite of our differences

Dodir Nade is an expression of the healing work of the church. This for me is summed up in Luke 4:18-19, when Jesus reads the prophet Isaiah in the synagogue:

The Spirit of the Lord is upon me,
   because he has anointed me
   to bring good news to the poor.
He has sent me to proclaim release to the captives
   and recovery of sight to the blind,
   to let the oppressed go free,
   to proclaim the year of the Lord's favour.

When I look back over my life, Dodir Nade has been the most significant and satisfying work I have ever undertaken. I have many happy memories of meeting so many people committed to working for peace. Sometimes the journeys themselves have been challenging, especially when we have had to run for trains and planes. We have worked in freezing temperatures and heat waves, but it has all been worth it. I am so thankful to be part of a programme of learning to live in a reconciling way.

The team relaxing in Osijek after a workshop
May 2022

Snježana with the giraffe and jackal
February 2023

Our workshop attendees at Ilok
February 2023

The restored Vukovar water tower re-opened in October 2020

The view over the Danube from the Water Tower in Vukovar

Epilogue

And finally, the last word must come from a workshop participant. Over the years, many have written their stories, generally containing something about their life history, experience of the war and of a Dodir Nade workshop. Out of the many, I have chosen Ana's. She attended our most recent cycle of workshops and does not wish her name to be changed.

My name is Ana and I was born on 10 July 1963, in Vukovar. The war caught me on the livestock farm where I was employed.

On 24 August 1991, when I came to work, due to the barricades around Vukovar, I couldn't return home. About 30 workers were stranded at the farm out of the 100 or so of us who were there at the time. The others (from May to August) had gone to Serbia, Bosnia and other parts of Croatia.

We worked together all day, listening to gunfire and explosions in Vukovar. In early October, the Yugoslav National Army (JNA) and territorial defence units entered the farm. They searched our apartments, moved into the empty ones, and restricted our movement. I went to work with military escort, guards were stationed at our workplaces. We went for informative talks, afraid to speak to each other.

On 6 November, me and five of my colleagues (Croats and Muslims) were tied up by the police and taken to Negoslavci. The moment when we walked bound through the farmyard is etched in my memory to this day. The army looked at us mockingly, my colleagues were silent, and I felt more humiliated than scared. In Negoslavci, we were imprisoned in a basement. I was physically and sexually abused there, but I survived. My colleagues were killed (one was found in the New Cemetery in Vukovar, and the others are still considered missing).

My feelings are divided. The first is fear and the desire not to exist, followed by anger. I thought, 'Why did this have to happen to me?' and, 'What kind of God allows such things?' After Negoslavci, I spent several days in Velepromet (a detention facility) and then until 21 December in Sremska Mitrovica, Serbia (in prison). I was exchanged then, and in Zagreb, I learned that my brother and several other family members had been killed. My mom never found out what happened to me. I tried to bury all the bad events deep inside me. I joined the Croatian Army. I felt protected, met my present husband, but in 1997, our baby died during childbirth. That's when the bad dreams, negative thoughts, and other traumas resurfaced. A psychiatrist diagnosed me with depression and PTSD. There were good days, but many more bad ones for me. Sometimes, it took a lot of strength just to get up and do something. I had my husband's support, as I do today, but there were times when we were silent and withdrew into ourselves.

In 2013, I started therapy with a group of women through the programme I Am More Than My Trauma, which helped me a lot, and my family was my greatest motivation and support. I realised my worth as a person, learned to communicate better with others, and solve problems. This program changed my life. That's why, when a close friend invited me to join the Touch of Hope workshops, I hesitated at first (I had never heard of the program before), but then I agreed to participate.

I view these workshops as an extension of the therapy I underwent 10 years ago. No matter how much you work on yourself, there are moments when life's problems and memories pull you back. I'm glad I went through these workshops.

The most significant thing I gained from this group is the empathy of the people who participated. I'm referring to the workshop leaders, but also to those who took part in the sessions. We come from different backgrounds, met for the first time, and gained so much good from each other. I feel a bit 'confined' as a person. That's why topics like communication, forgiveness and reconciliation are important to me. Something from each workshop has touched me. The fact that participants come from different regions helps me see some personal experiences from a different perspective. I also like how the leaders use biblical images to thoughtfully address various topics and apply them to resolving our different opinions. I believe the combination of their knowledge and our diversity led to successful work.

I try, and I hope I succeed, in applying what we've learned. It's important that I've learned to accept others as they are. Every problem is solvable if we deal with it. It's important to listen, not just hear other people, to avoid misunderstandings.

I thank the people who helped make this program a reality.

Questions for group discussion

Chapter 1 – Exploring health and healing

1   In small groups, draw a picture of what a healthy person looks like. What makes a person healthy? What is your definition of health?

2   Act out the story of the healing of the paralysed man as told in Mark 2:1-12. How does the story add to your understanding of health and healing?

3   What is the connection between personal healing and community reconciliation?

4   How do the exercises encourage the development of empathy and understanding between people?

Chapter 10 – Healthy communication

5   Think of an occasion when a person really listened to you. How did you feel? What made it a good experience?

6   Conversely, think of a time when you really wanted to share something important with a person but he or she did not listen to you in the way you wanted. How did that feel? What made it a bad experience?

7   Think of a conflict in which you have been, or are currently, involved. Look at the conflict through the means of non-violent communication. What observations are you making? What feelings are being expressed? What needs are not being met? What requests would you like to make?

8   How does the parable of the blind men and the elephant (page 101) relate to the challenges of communication and understanding in post-conflict settings?

9   Discuss how the power of language can both create division and foster healing.

Questions for group discussion

Chapter 11 – Identity

10   What is identity?

11   Draw and cut out the outline of a face. On one side print or draw signs and symbols that represent you. On the other side write and/or draw symbols that represent times when your identity has been threatened or hurt.

12   How do life's events challenge individuals to choose or prioritise certain aspects of their identity over others? What are the consequences of this?

13   How can individuals challenge their own stereotypes and promote empathy?

14   When religious identity becomes a point of conflict, how could it become one of unity?

Chapter 12 – The wounded healer

15 Think of a time when you have been hurt. How did you react? Are you still hurting? In what ways has healing happened or not?

16 Read the story of the Good Samaritan in Luke 10:25-37. Has there been a Good Samaritan in your life? The Samaritans were maligned by the Jews. Who are the Samaritans today in your community?

17 What does it mean to be 'present' with others, as described in the prayer for healing? How can this presence contribute to reconciliation?

18 What are the long-term effects of war on individuals and communities?

19 How can future generations be educated about past conflicts and their legacy in a way that promotes understanding and prevents and/or reduces the continuation of harm?

Questions for group discussion

Chapter 13 – Forgiveness

20 Read the story of Jo Berry and Pat Magee on the website theforgivenessproject.com What questions would you like to ask Jo Berry and Pat Magee? How do you feel about them both?

21 Archbishop Desmond Tutu in *The Book of Forgiving* offers us a Forgiveness Ritual to help us on an individual journey of forgiveness. If you are struggling to forgive a person, use the ritual yourself and note how you feel while using it.

22 How easy or difficult is it for you to forgive yourself?

23 Does forgiving a person mean the relationship is reconciled?

24 Does forgiveness have to be understood in terms of 'victim' and 'perpetrator'?

Chapter 14 – Living in a reconciling way

25 Think of a conflict situation. It could be something that has involved you or one you have observed. Listen out for the voices of Truth, Mercy, Justice and Peace? What are those voices saying?

26 What comes to mind when you hear the word 'reconciliation'?

27 In what ways can you create the space for reconciliation to happen in your community?

28 Having read the book, what issues have been raised for you? How will you take these forwards?

Books I have found helpful on my journey

Books about the former Yugoslavia and its subsequent break up

Bell, M *In Harm's Way* Penguin 1996 – a personal account by the BBC foreign affairs correspondent Martin Bell.

Collin, M *This is Serbia calling* Serpent's Tail 2001 – a book about the role of the media in the conflict.

Fowle, CR and Spiller, P *Wounded in War, Touched by Hope* Community for Reconciliation 2012 – stories from Dodir Nade participants.

Garrison, J *The Russian Threat* Gateway Books 1983.

Glenny, M *The Fall of Yugoslavia* Penguin 1996 – an excellent book about the early stages of the war in Croatia, including coverage of what happened in Eastern Slavonia.

Jegen, ME Sr *Sign of Hope* Life and Peace Institute 1996 – a lovely, readable account of the setting up of the Centre for Peace, Non-Violence and Human Rights in Osijek.

Judah, T *The Serbs* Yale University Press 1997 – a history of the Serbs.

Malcom, N. *Kosovo, a Short History* Papermac 1998 – a superb account.

Malcom, N. *Bosnia, a Short History* Papermac 1996 – an equally superb account.

Scott, A *Ottoman Odyssey* Riverrun 2019.

Šehić, F *Quiet flows the Una* Istros Books 2016 – a semi-autobiographical account of a soldier in the Bosnian war.

Tanner, M *Croatia, a Nation forged in War* Yale University Press 1997 – a history of Croatia.

West, R Black *Lamb and Grey Falcon* Canongate 2006 – a classic travel book about Yugoslavia, published in 1942 containing material about the history of the country. Be prepared for a long read.

In spite of our differences

Centre for Peace, Non-violence and Human Rights Osijek, editor Katarina Kruhonja, *I Choose Life* – a report on the first project phase 1998-2000.

Books on the themes on the Touch of Hope programme

Allport, G *Prejudice* – a classic book exploring a difficult theme.

Augsburger, DW *Helping People Forgive* Westminster John Knox Press 1996 – this book looks at the practice of forgiving.

Baum, G & Wells, H *The Reconciliation of Peoples* WCC 1997 – an analysis of the church's support (or lack of it) for reconciliation programmes.

Campbell, A *Rediscovering Pastoral Care* Darton, Longman and Todd 1981 – a helpful book exploring traditional models of pastoral care.

Curle, A *Another Way* Jon Carpenter 1995 – inspirational reading.

Curle, A *The Fragile Voice of Love* Jon Carpenter 2006.

Daniels, R *The Virgin Eye* Instant Apostle 2006 – an in-depth book on the spirituality of listening.

Elliott, C *Praying the Kingdom, towards a Political Spirituality* DLT 1985 – an excellent book on the spirituality of peace.

The Forgiveness Project, *The F Word: images of forgiveness*.

Fowle, CR *Stepping stones to reconciliation in the former Yugoslavia: Case study – The Bench We Share project* Department of Peace Studies Bradford University 1999 – my MA dissertation.

Halliday, J *Values and Principles for Mediation* – Mediation and Community Support.

Large, J *The War next door* Hawthorn Press 1997 – a critical look at the role of second track intervention in former Yugoslavia.

Lederach, JP *Reconcile* Herald Press 1999 – a very readable account of reconciliation and conflict resolution.

Books I have found helpful on my journey

Maalouf, A *On Identity* The Harvill Press 2000 – a readable account on this important subject.

Maddocks, M *The Christian Healing Ministry* SPCK 1981.

Mandela, N *Long walk to freedom*, Little Brown 1994.

Meyer, E *The Culture Map* Public Affairs 2015 – an excellent introduction to cultural differences.

Mitchels, B *Love in Danger* Jon Carpenter 2006 – an in-depth account of the life and work of Adam Curle.

Muller-Fahrenholz, G *The Art of Forgiveness* WCC Publications 1997 – an excellent book on Forgiveness from a German theologian.

Nouwen, HJM *The Wounded Healer* Darton, Longman and Todd 1996 – essential reading for wounded healers.

Nouwen, HJM *Peacework* Orbis Books 2005 – a book on the spirituality of peace.

Rosenberg, MB *Nonviolent Communication, A Language of Life* PuddleDancer Press 2003 – a masterly introduction to a different way of communicating.

Solnit, R *Hope in the Dark* Canongate 2005 – a helpful book for our times, on hope.

Stevens, D *The Land of Unlikeness* The Columba Press 2004 – a book about reconciliation from a former Leader of the Corrymeela Community.

Tokača, M *Signals of Heart* Research and Documentation Centre Sarajevo 2010 – positive stories from Bosnia and Herzegovina.

Tutu, D&M *The Book of Forgiving* William Collins 2014 – a helpful book on the practice of forgiveness.

Volf, M *Exclusion and Embrace* Abingdon 2019 – a scholarly book on the theology of reconciliation and identity.

Wilson, G with McCreary, A *Marie: A story from Enniskillen* Marshall Pickering 1991 – a moving account of Gordon Wilson who lost his daughter in the IRA attack at Enniskillen.

For more information

Touch of Hope is a programme of CfR Footprints (CfRFootprints.org), which operates under the auspices of the Community for Reconciliation, charity number 295113, company registration number 2041873 (GreenhouseatBarnesClose.org.uk)

> The Greenhouse at Barnes Close
> Chadwich Manor Estate
> B61 0RA

For up-to-date information contact Revd Clive Fowle – clivefowle1@gmail.com

For information on conflict support, conflict coaching, mediation and training, contact MACS (Mediation and Community Support) – mediationsupport.org.uk

www.ingramcontent.com/pod-product-compliance
Lightning Source LLC
Chambersburg PA
CBHW071240070526
44583CB00017B/2264